# EXPERIENCING GOD
# ALL WAYS
# AND EVERY DAY

*J. Norman King*

WINSTON PRESS

Library of Congress Catalog Card Number: 81-52350
ISBN: 0-86683-632-2

Printed in the United States of America

5   4   3   2   1

Winston Press, Inc., 430 Oak Grove,
Minneapolis, MN 55403

# EXPERIENCING GOD
## ALL WAYS
## AND EVERY DAY

*For Lorraine, Billy,*
*and Mary Katherine*

# Contents

# Preface

This book explores the view that God is the Presence we touch upon in our deepest human experience. The book is intended for a general audience, although it will be of interest to the specialist as well. It is directed to those who wrestle with the question of God, to those who are searching for a deeper meaning in their lives, whether their journey takes place inside or outside the boundaries of organized religion. It is hoped that this book will speak to their experience and will be helpful in their quest.

The question of God may be asked as three questions: Is God real? How can we experience God? How can we think and talk of God? These three questions are closely interrelated. For example, when we experience someone deeply in a human relationship, that person becomes real for us, and we form some image of what he or she is like. If we know of someone only through hearsay, we do not perhaps doubt that person's existence, but he or she will not make a difference in our lives. Similarly, we would expect that the experience of God would lead both to the conviction that God is real and to some image of who God is. But many people today find that commonly held ideas of God are far removed from the crucial events and issues of their lives. And so God has become somewhat unreal for them, even if they regard themselves as believers. The central challenge, therefore, is to discover whether it is possible to experience God today, to discover whether our vital experience does put us in touch with a transcendent reality. This book tries to address this challenge by spelling out one possible approach and by examining a number of basic human experiences.

The material in this book has emerged after considerable study, reflection, and struggle with a topic that has concerned me for many years. Many of its ideas were initially developed in preparation for classes taught at the University of Windsor. I am grateful to the students of those classes for their questions, comments, and discussions. I am also indebted to my colleagues in the Department of Religious Studies for the exchange of ideas, challenges, and support which have helped bring this work to completion.

The chief theological influence has been the thought of Karl Rahner. While Rahner's writings are at first somewhat forbidding, their breadth and depth of vision make a lasting impact. One senses in those writings the presence of profound truth that has been deeply experienced and carefully uttered. One goal of this book is to try to make Rahner's approach and some of his insights available to a wider public. Its ultimate goal, however, is to help deepen the sense of hope in all its readers.

On a more personal note, I am thankful to my parents for fostering an enduring interest in religious questions. I am grateful to my wife, Lorraine, for her overall support and her contribution to the content and style of this book, and to my young children, Billy and Mary Katherine, for the experience of gift and challenge that are the heart of life. A particular word of appreciation goes to Lloyd Meloche for many valuable conversations and for his encouragement during the unfolding of this work.

Thanks to John Kirvan, who acted as the initial contact with Winston Press. Special thanks to Cyril A. Reilly for his excellent editorial work, and to all the staff at Winston Press.

# PART ONE

# Perspectives

# CHAPTER ONE

# Introduction: Where Is Your God?

"Where is your God?" This question was asked long ago by Israel's skeptical neighbors at a time when the ancient Israelites were keenly feeling the absence of Yahweh and looking for some sign of his presence. Today we too are being asked: "Where can you point in real life and say, 'There you can find God'? Where can you show a genuine experience of this God? How do you know that God isn't just an empty word, a mere label, behind which you hide the inadequacies of your knowledge, your unfulfilled emotional needs, your anxiety in facing death? Does anything remain of your God after science has removed the illusions about nature and the human psyche which until now have been his hiding place?"

"Besides," people are saying, "there are more practical concerns. We have to survive, to keep up and improve our standard of living, to make sure we have all the good things in life. If you want to get involved in some higher cause, then look to all the economic and political problems in our

world. Don't waste time and energy thinking about something as intangible and unreal as God."

In these newer forms the ancient question confronts the
Christians of today. They too are a small group, scattered
throughout a world whose institutions and cultures are not
supportive of a specifically Christian orientation. What
reply, if any, is possible in this *diaspora* situation?

We will mention a number of different approaches
without demeaning them. Some people reply by echoing
the traditional formulas of faith. These problems, they say,
are mysteries we are not meant to understand but simply to
accept on faith. Others also repeat the familiar creeds, but
with an uneasiness they find hard to face. Some assert that
answers to all questions are to be found in the Bible. Others
cling in desperation to a biblical language and world which
no longer seem quite real. Still others point to a highly
emotional experience of conversion as the basis of their
assurance. With such an experience alone, they claim,
come understanding and certainty; outside its bounds lie
only ignorance and confusion. Many people today have left
behind all formal religious ties and have yet to find a vision
which helps them to make sense of their lives.

All these ways have their merits, but they do not seem to
satisfy us. Why does each of them fall short? Simply to
avoid the question of God seems intellectually dishonest. It
may mask a hidden fear that if we bring our convictions
into the clear light of day, they may evaporate into nothing
because they are without foundation. Or we may see them
as precious but vulnerable; we fear the loss of something
we do not know how to defend. Yet if we just repeat
doctrinal formulas and biblical phrases we are left with
hollow-sounding words unconnected to the way we con-

cretely live and experience and think. The words easily become unreal, and so does the God of whom they allegedly speak.

A highly emotional experience of conversion is extremely vivid and real. Yet it too may contain elements of illusion and self-deception. It may be brief and passing and touch only a small, superficial part of our being. A desire for feelings of well-being and security may cloak a fear of deeper truth. Here God does not become unreal but may cease to be God by being reduced to a human feeling. On the other hand, to abandon all religious ties may not lead us to a fuller truth. What we are looking for may lie hidden beneath former beliefs and practices.

To put it starkly, is there any alternative to evasion, mere words, surface emotionalism, or outright dismissal of the question of God? Any worthwhile approach will have to respond directly to the question "Where is your God?" and so must point to the experience of God. But it must penetrate beneath the surface to the deepest levels of human experience and do so with a probing, open mind. Our question then becomes: Is there anything we touch upon in our deepest experience to which the word "God" might correspond? What are the most suitable ideas and words to express and interpret this experience?

Karl Rahner is one theologian who confronts this challenge, and his thought has been a guiding force throughout this work. While the discussion presented here is my own, it draws upon many concerns central to Rahner's work: his attempts to link religious and Christian concepts to human experience, his treatment of the unique experience of God as accessible to all, and his delineation of certain avenues of that experience. (See his *Foundations of Christian Faith*.)

For Rahner the question of God is *the* human question,

and it reflects a quest arising from the inmost heart of every human person. Rahner maintains, too, that everyone does experience the reality we call God. Yet, he adds, many overlook or fail to recognize that experience. It may remain vague and without a word or a name. On the other hand, we are well aware that people do carry with them images of God inherited from their childhood, their religious instruction, or their cultural ambiance. They may even accept these images as true. The images, however, are often cut off from any living roots and no longer capture anything real in their daily lives.

We appear then to have both an experience of God without a name and, on the other hand, names for God that have no experience behind them. How is it possible to have an experience we cannot think or talk about and to have ideas and words we cannot join to any experience? As we will illustrate, it is possible because of the peculiar nature of the experience of God. This is not just one particular experience which can be neatly parceled and set in a row alongside others. It is a special dimension of every human experience, but it is obscure and elusive and hence can go unnoticed. It is like something that is always there but is never seen or heard unless we look or listen in the right way.

So our task is twofold: (1) to uncover and name the universal experience of God and (2) to show how traditional images and doctrines do relate to this experience.

This task is vital at the present time. We live in an age in which people strongly feel the absence of God. We look out upon a pluralistic, secularized, technological world and find nothing that speaks to us of God. Only our own image stares back at us from the world we ourselves have fashioned. But that image tastes of our own finiteness. It reminds us, whether in architectural beauty or in crumbling concrete, of the birth and death of ourselves and of all we touch. This finiteness pains us and reveals a deep longing for something more.

This longing is an undercurrent flowing through our entire lives and thrusting us onward in all we say and do. But it breaks forth to the surface of our awareness more irresistibly in the crucial events, stages, and situations of our lives. Some may contend that this longing is futile. But if it is not in vain and if our life is not just a pointless quest after shadows, then the "something more" is real. In what follows we will attempt to illustrate that the "something more" to which we reach, within yet beyond all we encounter, is what is meant by the word "God." In this process we seek neither to undermine people's cherished convictions nor to compel their unwilling assent. We simply invite the reader to consult and reflect on his or her own experience and to consider whether the interpretation offered speaks to that experience and provides a reasonable understanding of it.

Many people today do indeed suspect that we stand over a yawning chasm of nothingness, a chasm only thinly covered by our daily routine. They think it better not to probe, better to keep busy so as to distract themselves from the pain of such awareness. It is urgent, therefore, to spell out the experience of God as "something more" rather than a mere void, and to try to direct people toward that experience so that they may begin to discover hope or give their hope a new or renewed voice.

The chief avenues which open onto this elusive reality will be those key moments or dimensions of life in which our whole self is involved or at stake. These include silence in solitude, responsible freedom, generous love, death and enduring meaning, social involvement, guilt and forgiveness, and the like. In such moments we catch a clearer glimpse of the longing which permeates our existence and of the mystery toward which it tends. In this book we will explore a number of these pathways to God.

In Part One we will try to mark out a framework within which these experiences may be viewed. This effort is utterly essential. It is akin to constructing the kind of glasses through which we look at these experiences. Whether we look with rose-colored or dark-colored lenses, for example, is very important. Even more vital is the angle from which we view these experiences. Both the kind of glasses and the way we look through them will greatly affect what we see and how we interpret it. To use another image, providing this framework is like forming the skeleton upon which the flesh of our experiences will be layered and contoured. This task may perhaps seem as dry as the bones Ezekiel writes about, but it is just as necessary. We begin by showing that the core of Christianity is precisely this basic, universal experience of God (Chapter 2). We next distinguish the experience of God from the so-called proofs of God (Chapter 3) and spell out its fundamental characteristics (Chapter 4). We will then be better equipped to discover God as that ineffable mystery we encounter in our deepest human experience (Part Two, or Chapters 5-10).

# CHAPTER TWO

# The Core
# of Christianity

To speak of a core of Christianity and to relate it to a
universal experience of God may strike us as a little
strange. After all, Christianity may well appear to be just
one small body of opinion, lost in a sea of competing and
conflicting world views and life-styles. Even within the
spectrum of Christianity there is a wide range of views
and emphases which seem scarcely reconcilable with one
another.

Each of the long-established denominations itself ex-
hibits a mass of doctrinal and moral teachings, a litany of
sacramental and liturgical rites and devotional practices,
and a maze of institutional structures. How is it possible to
make sense of all this detail, let alone relate it to our lives?

Rahner states that for all Christianity's complexity, its
nucleus is very simple. At its heart is the experience of
God, which it interprets in a particular way. Christianity
simply says that what we touch upon in our deepest
experience may be best described (in limited human terms)

as the self-bestowing nearness of forgiving love. Every-thing else is nothing but an elaboration of this core, from which it flows and to which it leads back (*Christian at the Crossroads,* pp. 31-36).

We may begin our own uncovering of this core through an illustration taken from human friendship. It may be a little too anthropomorphic, but it can be refined as we go along.

What do we do in giving ourselves to another? We take something of our self—a thought, a conviction, a fear, a hope, an interest. We wrap it up, so to speak, in a word or an action. Then we offer it to the other. To the extent that any of us is able to put our self into a word or action, it contains us. And it does so in a way that can be heard or seen or touched. Something spiritual or interior is given flesh, body. It is made incarnate, symbolized.

To the degree that the other is open, this word or action will strike home. It will find its way to the very heart of the other and call forth a response from that deep level. The result is a sharing of what is alive within the persons, a communication that is literally life-giving.

The most complete instance of this process would occur if we were able to gather all that we are and all that we have and put it into one word (or action), and speak this word from the heart. This word would embody our very self. Presuming the other's complete openness, it would pene-trate to his or her very heart and evoke a total response. The result would be a total sharing of life.

While recognizing the limitations and noting the biblical flavor of this analogy, we may use it to get at the essence of Christianity. We start with a question which carries our earlier query a little further. Do we find anywhere a word which fully expresses or gives flesh to what we encounter in our deepest human experience, in a way that strikes to our very heart and brings something to life in us? Do we find anywhere a life-giving word of God?

According to the Christian tradition, we do find such a word in Jesus. He is the one who addresses the mystery as "Father" and whose "Spirit" dwells in our hearts so that we may have life in its fullness. Briefly phrased, the ultimate reality (Father) speaks a Word (incarnate Son) which penetrates to the human heart and remains there as presence (Spirit). As with Lazarus (John 11), this word cuts through any deadness that envelopes us, touches the center of our being, and calls us forth to life. The basic Christian doctrines of Trinity, Incarnation, and grace are here stated in a way that relates to and interprets our experience of "something more." Let us continue to unfold this image.

Jesus is the Word which expresses God in a way we can touch. He embodies or incarnates the reality we designate as "God." As a Word spoken *to us,* he is a gift to us, just as our own words contain the gift of our self to another. He thereby conveys the truth that what is deepest in existence, God, can be described as giving, as self-bestowing. He also portrays the final source from which he is uttered as "Father," that is, as generative source of life. This source is not a void or a destructive force from which humans are randomly spewed forth as driftwood. It is life-germinating, life-fostering.

As *total* incarnation of this mystery, Jesus is the Word of God in which everything is uttered and cannot be called back. He is the living symbol of this divine self-giving that is total and irrevocable. The gift is lasting and can always be counted upon. The self-bestowing reality may therefore be

depicted as trustworthy. This is perhaps what the traditional language means when it speaks somewhat abstractly
of the immutability of God or more concretely of the
fidelity of God.

This Word progressively unveils itself in the life, death,
and resurrection of Jesus. We are thus told that the
self-giving, trustworthy mystery at the heart of all reality
is not only life-furthering but generates life even out of
death. In the many deaths in the midst of life that are
caused by sickness, failure, loss, and the like, we are
summoned to hope for newness of life. With Job we are
called to affirm: "Even though he slay me, still shall I trust
him" (Job 13:15). The right word for the God of our
experience is therefore Jesus. In Jesus what is meant by
"God" is embodied and offered. It is to be discovered in his
body which is given for us.

As a word which contains and offers the whole "self" of
God, this Word does strike to the heart of us humans. Like
the biblical two-edged sword, it pierces through to the very
center of our being. There the Word remains as a life-
giving presence. As present in our inmost depths, this mystery
is called "Spirit" or "Holy Spirit." What is silently there in
our inner sanctuary is precisely what is voiced in the Word.
It is that which bestows itself as source of life, even life out
of death. This is a way of viewing what is meant by "grace."

If we journey to the center of our being we find not just a
dark and vacant place but a dwelling filled with a life-giving
light. We discover, in fact, not just ourselves but the
"something more" for which we are searching. The discovery of God is the discerning of a presence, a something
which is already there. "Spirit" designates this presence at
the core of our being.

When another person makes his or her presence felt in our heart through words, that person invites our response so that life may be shared and enhanced. If we depict Spirit as the inner presence of the Word of God, what shape would such an invitation assume? How do we actually experience such a summons to respond? It is felt precisely as that undercurrent of longing for "something more" which pervades our entire lives. We may describe it as a hunger, unsatiated by anything we directly encounter, for a fullness of life, even out of the many deaths we undergo.

"Faith" may be regarded as the assurance that this longing is not in vain but can be trusted. Faith then is the conviction, gratefully held, that our deepest longing does not betray us but puts us in touch with the most real truth about human existence. What is present at the core of our being, yet beyond us, is a trustworthiness which, as the old act of faith phrased it, can neither deceive nor be deceived. In the words of St. Paul, it is the Spirit of the Son dwelling in our hearts which makes us call out to the Father (Romans 5:15 and 8:15).

If we look then to our inmost center and furthest outreach as human persons, we will be led to the divine reality. If we scan human history for some indication, some sign, some concrete incarnation of what we encounter in our deepest experience, and if in our search we come across the man Jesus, then we might be able to say, "This is the right word. This is the true word which gives flesh to what is within my heart and beyond it, to what is at once given and still hoped for." God is the presence within (Spirit) which is totally other (Father) and embodied in Jesus (Son).

We may add one further thought before gathering up

these reflections. To speak of Jesus as Word of God is not merely to speak of one word which might be arbitrarily chosen from a number of possibilities. Nor does it mean that his being human is only incidental to his being such a word. It is *as* a human being and *as* this particular human being that Jesus is Word of God. The human person is not just a somewhat bizarre offshoot of a mindlessly chaotic universe. Nor is he or she merely an arbitrary product of a kind of divine *fiat.* On the contrary, the human being is what comes to be if the infinite reality, God, is expressed in finite terms. In *Theological Investigations,* vol. 4 (p. 116), Rahner says it this way: "If God wills to become non-God, man comes to be, that and nothing else."

The right word, the symbol or image of God, is the human being. If we wish to know what God is like in human terms, we must look to the express image of God. The countenance of the Infinite shines forth in every human person, however obscurely. The word of God is uttered in every human being, however haltingly. The full light and the complete word are found in the man Jesus. He is thus called *the* light and *the* word—the way and the truth and the life (John 14:6). Nevertheless, this light does shine and this word does speak in everyone who comes forth into the world.

Because of this intrinsic bond between the divine and the human, statements about God and human beings are bound up together. We cannot speak of God without speaking of human beings; we cannot speak theologically about human beings without speaking of God. If we look at our human longing from the heart, we must speak of God as that from which and to which it reaches. If we try to talk of God, we also talk of that which is before and beyond our outreach. We refer to the ground of our self and the horizon of our hope. We speak in terms of our longing. Again, the human face of God is the human being itself. But that human face is one that looks toward God.

We may now perhaps sketch an initial response, in Christian terms, to our question "Where is your God?" or "Where do you find God?" God is here as Spirit at the core of our being. If we follow the path of solitary silence which leads to our inmost depths, there we will find God. At the same time, God is likewise incarnate in our world in the man Jesus. God is present in the man for others and in all the others for whom this man is. If we go out of ourself to the other and follow the path of personal caring and social responsibility, there too we will find God. However, what we will discover in our own self and in our neighbor is not just ourself and our neighbor: We will discover the totally transcendent who is named Father. In our solitude and in our love we will find God. But what we will find is beyond all solitude and all love.

From a Christian viewpoint, God is what we touch upon in our deepest human experience. We touch here not an empty abyss but a self-bestowing source of the fullness of life even out of death. God is the presence within at the core of our being which is totally other and embodied in the man Jesus. God as immanent is Spirit; God as transcendent is Father; God as incarnate is Son.

# CHAPTER THREE

# Experience Versus Proofs of God

In this chapter we want to show briefly how the experience of God and the so-called proofs for the existence of God are both distinct and related. We begin by looking at the difference between what we experience and what we are able to put into words. In doing so we draw upon and adapt the thoughts of Karl Rahner. (See especially *Foundations,* pp. 68-71, and *Theological Investigations,* vol. 11, pp. 149-165.)

We might on occasion see a film, read a book, converse with someone, or witness a birth or a death which really grips us. While there is an immediate impact, its meaning may dawn on us only later, sometimes even years later, in a way that we can express in words. Observe a child learning to speak. "Hot" describes a vividly painful sensation in the fingers when one touches certain objects. "Gone" refers to something that has disappeared down one's stomach or otherwise vanished from sight. "Bunny" is the soft smooth thing one drags around the house and holds while sleeping.

For a child, a word is a label on an experience. The word draws that experience out of the surrounding blur of impressions and feelings and focuses it. As in the creation story of Genesis, the word is a creative way of bringing order out of chaos. An idea or word helps to capture an experience, at least partially.

So we need to distinguish between how we experience something and how we later put the experience into thoughts and words. We experience joy and sorrow, fear and trust, thought and decision, before we pause to reflect upon them. And there is always more to lived experience than we can say, even if we have remarkable philosophic and poetic gifts. We are nevertheless impelled to reflection and expression. We thereby deepen the original experience and develop our understanding.

We may of course deny the experience or let it atrophy. We may try to banish a gnawing anxiety from our mind or let a sensitivity to beauty lie dormant for lack of support from our environment. We may also interpret an experience poorly or wrongly. We may fail to find the right words, or we may place the experience in a wrong perspective. We may stumble in our attempts to convey an overwhelming insight, or we may mistake a transient emotional attachment for love.

The so-called proofs for the existence of God should be seen in the light of this distinction between experience and its interpretive concept or word. These proofs are really an effort to articulate our more primordial experience of God. They are neither possible nor meaningful apart from that experience. At the same time, we are dealing with experience of a unique kind. While this experience is inescapably present in everyone, interpreting it at the philosophical and theological level is extremely difficult. It is important at the outset, then, to point out and overcome certain inadequacies and errors that can easily arise.

Once again, this inquiry does not seek to throw out anything crucial to the question of God, but to see the issue in a new light. For both believers and non-believers, reflection on God can be very disturbing. An example taken from human relationships may be useful here. When we begin to see someone close to us in a new light, our familiar image is shaken and the relationship may appear threatened. But if our new awareness is truer, it can establish a deeper, more realistic bond. Likewise, if we see the issue of God in a fuller light, initial misgivings and anxieties may also give way to stronger convictions.

The question of God is commonly asked in this fashion: "How do I know there is a God, and how does this God fit into my life?" This approach can readily go astray, because its starting place and way of asking are questionable. It readily presumes that we already know what the term "God" means and that we merely have to determine whether God exists or not. This approach may simply take for granted a highly doubtful image of God.

People have often tended to think of God as one particular being we have encountered alongside others in our world. While he was certainly considered the highest entity, he was in fact pictured as one among many others. He was regarded as the ruler of all, who intervened dramatically from time to time in the sphere of nature or human history to set things right. It has become increasingly difficult for many to believe in this kind of cosmic-engineer God or social-planner God. Perhaps we at least dimly recognize that our image of God cannot be so facilely carved. If God is at all real, God must be more silently unfathomable and awesome.

This customary approach is also inclined to assume that we are trying to prove the existence of an external being, an outsider, of whom we have previously heard little or nothing and with whom we have never dealt. It is as though we have had no experience of God before his existence and relevance were demonstrated in words. The proofs then seem like an attempt to convince someone of a truth which has had no previous bearing upon his or her life—like establishing the existence of a remote land to which we have never traveled and with which we have no ties. Such an attempt may be a matter of idle curiosity, but it is unlikely to be of crucial concern. In this view, God remains a stranger who has to be brought into our lives from outside. Such a God always comes too late— already removed from what is deepest and most vital in our lives.

The question of God is not, therefore, an inquiry about one possible being among others, whom we might (or might not) come across in our journey through life, and who is only then introduced as an outsider into our experience, thought, and decision.

On the contrary, the alleged proofs of God should be looked upon as the unveiling of a presence which is already there at the heart of life and reality whether or not we recognize, overlook, or deny this presence. These proofs simply attempt to bring more clearly to our mind a reality which is actually experienced and at least dimly glimpsed and implicitly decided about. They strive to make us aware that always and everywhere the human person does have dealings with God, whether or not he or she reflects upon it, admits it, or even uses the word "God."

The proofs are not, then, like a mathematical deduction which reaches a conclusion in a detached, impersonal way about something novel and unfamiliar. They resemble more the process of a deepening self-understanding in which there is a dawning recognition of something we have always somehow known. What once remained in the background is now brought forward into clearer relief and sheds new light on everything. In a therapeutic conversation, for example, whether between friends or in a professional setting, the right word can capture and illuminate confused emotions, vague thoughts, or conflicting values. What we did actually know, but could not pin down or find words for, leaps into awareness. It has a ring of truth which resonates deeply within us even though we might never have thought of it or said it in that way.

In this context, "God" is the right word for that which we encounter in our deepest human experience. However, we must not refer to this experience and then conclude "Therefore there is a God," as if we knew explicitly and precisely beforehand what the term meant. Rather, we strive to point to this experience and then say: "This is what is meant by 'God.'" In other words, the concept of God must be rooted in and give expression to the experience of God. The experience comes first.

Where do we look for the experience of God? We may focus this question in the light of an earlier example. Does the child experience God before he or she has learned the word? If we answer no, the word has no foothold or anchor in the child's life. At most it may be linked to an infantile image of the parent. This may shackle the child in misconceptions from which he or she may never escape, even as an adult. If we reply yes, we must locate the experience of the child to which the term "God" relates. If we cannot answer the question in the case of the child, it is not likely that our own concepts of God are rooted in anything real in our lives. Is there an experience that pervades our lives from birth to death? Yes. It is the reaching out for "something more." We have already spoken of this "self-transcendence" of the human person. We may now examine it a little more closely, with reference to the basic human quest for meaning. The next chapter will consider its basic characteristics.

A person is a questioning being. This is so in two senses. We are beings who ask questions, and we are questing beings. We reach out in thought and in desire, with our mind and with our will. This tendency is evident in the endless queries of the small child and in his or her relentless efforts to walk, talk, explore and relate—modified, as in the adult, by a certain trepidation. Yet however great our knowledge and insight, we never reach a completion which brings an end to inquiring. Nor in all we choose and love do we ever find a final resting place. A deep longing in our soul remains unstilled. For every answer there is a further question. We go through life with questions which reach further than any answers we receive.

Our questioning, moreover, concerns not just this or that object outside us but our very selves as well. We must ask who we are and what we are for. A little girl, for example, asks "Where did I come from?" She is not seeking a technical reply. She wants to be told a story in which she is a central character and made to feel that she is welcomed into the family and makes a difference there. She is really asking: "Am I important? Do I belong?" We too seek a sense of worth and belonging. We are confronted with our own identity and purpose as a question. It is not intellectually but by the way we live our life that we respond to the question of its meaning.

Like the child, we look back to the past and imagine or project ourselves into the future. We are aware that our life began and that it will come to an end. We are aware of our birth and are increasingly faced with the fact of our coming death. As a result, we can envisage our life as a whole. We are thereby led to ask about its meaning as a whole. In addition, we are not just self-contained and isolated entities. Our self, even in its uniqueness, emerges from and is bound up with a complex network of things and persons which form our environment. The strands of our self also reach out into a past and a future broader than our own and of which we are a part. And so we ask as well about the meaning of all that is, of the whole of reality.

This question of total meaning pursues us even though we may try to hide or run away from it. It may arise, for instance, in a moment of anxiety when a familiar bond is shattered or a cherished ideal turns to dust and everything seems to fall away, leaving us all alone in a bottomless darkness, threatened and helpless in our very self. It may occur forcefully when we are faced with a vocational or occupational decision, where the whole future course of our life and even the kind of person we are to become appear to be decisively at stake. It may come too in a moment of despair, when it strikes us that our whole past life has been a mistake and our present life appears to be slipping through our fingers toward an equally empty future. Conversely, at a moment of intense joy or peace or closeness to another we may be overwhelmed by the conviction that life is indeed radically sacred and good.

The very experience of life itself, with its fragility, loneliness, contingency, and death, can evoke in us a sense of weariness, emptiness, darkness, and despair. We may wonder if life is not after all absurd and meaningless. Yet we encounter a great deal of truth, goodness, courage, honesty, love, and joy. These call forth a basic trust in life's meaningfulness. There is a puzzling and often painful ambiguity here.

The fragments of our life are like the beads of a necklace, the pieces of a puzzle, or the elements of a story. We wonder if there is a unifying thread, a total picture, a complete story which fits or ties everything together. We ask about and long for a final meaningfulness to the whole of life, one that envelopes, reconciles, integrates, and surpasses all the individual meanings and absurdities. It is in the experience of this asking and longing for final meaningfulness that we grasp implicitly what is meant by "God."

The proofs of God enter at this point. They spring from and try to interpret this experience and make it explicit. They flow from our experience of ourselves as questioning beings. They try to spell out what our experience presupposes and what it implies. Let us attempt to do so briefly at this point.

Our questioning is a reaching out of and beyond ourselves. Yet it arises from so deeply within us that it could be said to characterize or define us more than anything else does. To put it in pictorial form: We stand with our whole self, our entire life, in our inquiring and striving hands. And we wonder: What, if anything, do we stand upon? What, if anything, do we reach toward? Do we merely

hover at a brink over which we will eventually plunge into
an abyss of nothingness? Do our reaching fingers simply
trail off into a void? Do we stand upon and reach for
something, or for nothing? Are the ground upon which
our self and its questioning rest and the term or goal toward
which it reaches nothing, or something? A void, or a
presence? Does the search for total meaningfulness pro-
ceed from nothing to nothing, or from something to
something? These are the stark alternatives. In Rahner's
view this ground and term must be something, must be
reality, for nothing cannot be the ground of something. If
the striving is real, so too must be its ground and goal. In
this perspective the ground and goal of this deeply rooted
longing for total meaning is what is meant by "God."

The word "God," therefore, would designate the basis
and goal of the meaningfulness of life and reality, that upon
which it rests and toward which it tends. We thus experience God implicitly as both the source from which we flow
as meaning-seeking beings and as the goal toward which we
tend as the fulfillment of that meaning. We implicitly
decide about and respond to God, positively or negatively,
by accepting or rejecting the meaningfulness of our own
life. We do so of course by the fundamental direction we
give to our life rather than by just our isolated thoughts
or actions.

Here again we simply invite readers to consult their own
experience. Perhaps they will find that they are sometimes
dragged down by a feeling of futility, a sense that life
is after all pointless. But this experience hurts so much
that we shield the last flicker of hope rather than ex-
tinguish its light. Or if we look with any degree of love
at our young children whose lives are unfolding in our

presence, our every instinct rebels against the thought that their lives are without meaning. It *is* possible—though sometimes difficult—to be convinced that life has meaning.

We may possibly realize too that this conviction is not one we can readily pick up or discard. Meaning is something we discover rather than invent, something we reach for but cannot confer upon ourselves. To experience meaning, then, is to experience a source from which it flows. We also recognize that to believe in God while holding that life is absurd, is a contradiction. No creed affirms the creator of a meaningless heaven and earth. So the experience of meaning and the belief in God are bound up together. It seems reasonable, therefore, to envisage God as the ultimate source and goal of experienced meaning.

To put it very simply, a person who experiences life as meaningful is filled with a profound gratitude and drawn toward a responsible generosity. In effect, such a person experiences life as a gift, accepts the gift, and assumes responsibility for it. That from which we flow as gift and toward which we are grateful and responsible is what is meant by "God."

The experience of God is therefore implicit in the experience of meaning. When this experience of meaning is intellectually articulated, we have what are known as the proofs of God. When it is embodied in action that is in accordance with the unconditional demands of one's conscience, we have its moral articulation. When it is expressed in a doctrinal, liturgical, and organizational manner, we have institutional religion. And when the latter is given its fullest articulation, we have (from a consciously Christian standpoint) explicit Christianity.

In all these levels we must also recognize that the experience of God is public and social, since all human experience, even the most intimately interior, occurs within a physical and cultural environment comprising other things and especially other persons.

We will now explore further this experience of what we will call mystery, which is found in but is distinct from its intellectual, moral, and institutional expression.

## CHAPTER FOUR

# The Experience of God as Mystery

God is what we touch upon in our deepest human experience, the experience of reaching beyond ourselves from the heart for "something more." It is a reaching for a meaningfulness for our whole life and for all of reality. God is both the source and the goal of this meaningfulness. We will now look a little more closely at this mystery from which we flow and toward which we reach. We will do so in terms of our knowledge and freedom, that is, our outreach of mind and will. "Mystery" does not refer here to something presently unknown which has still to be figured out and mastered. We use the term to point, rather, to a reality which is experienced but whose inexhaustible depths and breadth our powers can never encompass.

We noted earlier that what we directly know and love does not respond fully to our mind and will in a way that puts an end to our inquiring and longing. But what *do* we directly encounter, and why does it fall short?

We look at a tree or an automobile, a cat or a cloud, a

smiling or a stern face, or a painting of any of these. We
hear the sound of the wind and of thunder, the laughter,
weeping, and shouting of persons, the din of traffic, the
chatter of the mass media, the flow of music, the silence
before dawn. As we smell and taste, touch and feel such
things, we are aware of ourselves as doing so. We experience ourselves as a kind of center to whom these impressions come. We are aware too that it is somewhat within
our power to respond in one way or another to these
impressions. In this sense at least we are free.

We are physical beings, and our direct contact is with
what we can see and hear and touch, taste and smell—the
persons and things whose bodiliness impinges upon our
senses. We have a kinship with the animals, plants, and
minerals with which we share this planet and upon which
we rely for sustenance. At the same time we are curiously
endowed with self-awareness and freedom. We are, so to
speak, matter that can understand and care. We belong to
and live in an environment of both nature and culture. Our
dwelling place is a physical realm of space, time, and
bodiliness, inextricably interwoven with the more distinctly human world of work and technology, art and
friendship, society and community.

This is the world we directly know and within which we
make our choices. We fashion our images, concepts, and
words from this world. We decide and act, too, with
reference to the things and persons we meet in the daily
round of our lives. Yet a kind of restless yearning permeates all these ventures, leaving us never fully satisfied.
From the dawning of our lives, when we cry out for food
and companionship, we gradually realize that no particular
gift we receive, no achievement in word or deed, no person

we meet or grow close to, can fill this deep longing within us. There is a kind of untouched loneliness in each human being that no other can fully reach.

No limited being we know or choose fills the whole expanse of our mind and will. We receive all we know into a mind whose scope is wider than anything it contains. The embrace of our desire, too, is always wider than anything it enfolds. The reason is that we see everything in the light of something more or vaster, and we choose everything in view of that something more. What, then, is the narrowness of all we encounter directly? And what, by contrast, is the breadth of our outreach?

All things and all persons fall short because they are finite. They are fragile and perishable and, in a basic sense, gratuitous, unnecessary. In consequence, they are not enough, singly or together. This is true of ourselves as well. Behind our need to reach out lies a sense of our own incompleteness and vulnerability. We therefore experience ourselves and our world as finite and contingent. On occasion we even do so with a vivid starkness that jars and unnerves us.

Here a striking question arises: How do we know that we and our world are finite? We can know finite things without precisely knowing that they are finite. The infant, for example, knows her parents and relates to them. Only later, however, does she recognize that what she has been doing all along is relating and that the persons to whom she has been relating are her parents. She knows this reality only when she has acquired a broader experience and is able to think and speak in a more sophisticated manner. She then has a context within which to place this particular experience.

To know something as finite or limited is likewise possible only if we see it within a wider context. This must be the context of infiniteness. (This is a central contention of Rahner, and in the next few pages we will try to simplify and concretize his perspective.) We can know a limit as such only if we have somehow gone beyond it, at least in thought or intention. To know that there is a fence around a given field, we must be able to see beyond that fence; we must see the field as enclosed within a larger area. To grasp all we encounter as finite, limited, or "fenced in," we must see it within the wider context of the infinite or limitless. In our attempts to go beyond the fence, we may bump against it. Our "bumping against" the finite fails to end our inquiring because our mind's basic drive is toward the infinite.

It remains true that we directly know only the things and persons we contact with our senses. But we meet them as finite, and we know it. We can know them as finite only because in knowing them we hold them up, as it were, to the light of the infinite and weigh them accordingly. Yet we do not directly know the infinite. We are aware of it only by a kind of background awareness present in the act of knowing anything finite, a little like knowing the night sky only as the backdrop against which we see the stars.

To clarify this elusive matter, we may call further attention to a distinction which is crucial for interpreting the experience of God. As in the above examples of the child-parent bond and the enclosed field, we may distinguish between what we see and how we see it. Several persons, for instance, may look at rain falling. For one it may spell renewed hope for a parched crop. For others it may mean a spoiled picnic, or puddles to splash in, a peaceful sound, or a slight inconvenience. Or again, suppose a child is born. This new life may evoke an overwhelming joy and sense of life's mystery. But it may also be felt as an additional burden to care for, a by-product of careless sexual activity, a reminder of one's own vanished promise, or a profound and creative responsibility. In each of the examples, what is known is the same, but its context or the horizon against which it is known is vastly different from the other contexts or horizons.

Our awareness includes, therefore, not only what we immediately observe but the horizon or background against which we observe it. We often make this distinction without thinking about it. We complain, for example, that a certain person sees things only in terms of his or her own needs and wants and is blind to anyone else's point of view. A horizon is like the kind of glasses through which we view things. Or it is the angle of vision, frame of reference, point of view, or perspective with which we approach, understand, and assess the facts, events, situations, and relationships of our lives.

We do, of course, have many horizons through which we approach life. We may look at situations in terms of how they affect our business, our family, our image in the eyes of others. Our horizons can be broad or narrow, clear or confused. We may try to view every subsequent happening in our life as the offshoot of some early childhood occurrence. Or a friend's outlook on life may help us to understand better our own inner conflicts.

Our horizons often remain in the background of our awareness. To become explicitly aware of a horizon as such, we must get beyond it; we must see it in a still wider context. Then we can determine whether this horizon has helped us to see clearly or has distorted our vision. This can be a painful process, since we may discover that for all too long we have been looking at something in the wrong way. However, an essential part of mental growth consists precisely in acquiring new horizons, better angles of vision with which to view reality. In the realm of science this process involves developing a model, paradigm, or hypothesis which better accounts for the data.

To carry matters a step further, we can try to imagine one horizon wider than all the others. It would be contained by no other horizon, but encompass all of them. This would be the final horizon against which all else is seen. If we experience everything we directly encounter as finite, it is because we see everything against an infinite horizon. The infinite is the widest and final horizon. All that we directly know is seen in its light. In another image, the infinite is like a limitless field which contains yet stretches endlessly beyond all our finite objects and frameworks.

We cannot look directly at the infinite. The infinite is like a light behind us which shines on everything and in whose light all else is seen. Without it we would see nothing at all, but it is not itself directly seen. It could also be pictured as the background screen against which all else is projected and viewed but which is not itself directly seen or noticed.

God is always thought of as infinite or transcendent. Our preceding discussion is one way of portraying that infiniteness. From this standpoint, God is seen as the mystery of infinite light which floods and envelopes all our awareness of the finite things and persons which make up our world. God is the infinite "something more" for which our questioning mind searches as it looks out upon the finite world. Of all we directly know, we implicitly say "This is not God." Of all we directly know we implicitly ask "Where is God?"

We have considered the outreach of our mind. Let us now examine the longing of our will for this infinite mystery we call "God."

To know ourselves and all that is before us as finite carries with it a certain disappointment. Everything finite fails to fill the profound longing in our being, the depth and vastness of our desire. There remains an emptiness, a sense of something missing, because our inmost longing is for the infinite. Only the infinite can touch and fill the lonely expanse of our yearning.

This truth is perhaps best illustrated in the difference between the many hopes we may have and the underlying sense of hope. We may hope for many specific things: a house or car, a creative occupation, a loving husband or wife. Yet no concrete attainment ever exhausts our hope or quenches the thirst within us. Each attainment becomes a stepping-stone or launching-point for something else. Our hope always outruns our hopes. Conversely, all our specific hopes can be dashed without our necessarily losing hope: The sense of hope can be stronger than even the most drastic loss. So neither the gain nor the loss of anything finite can of itself sustain or destroy our hope, because all our hopes are finite, while the basic goal of our hope is the infinite.

The infinite is thus that "something more" toward which our whole being tends from its inmost center, in mind and will alike. This orientation is not free. It is, however, the very basis of our freedom. Nothing we directly touch fully answers the orientation of our will; hence nothing can compel our response. Our response remains optional, a matter of choice. Since no finite creature is quite what we are looking for, it is thus possible to pass it by.

The immense human longing, however, is not just an appetite for receiving. Nor is freedom merely a matter of looking for objects to fill up our emptiness. In a fuller sense, to be explored later, a person's freedom concerns the capacity to give himself or herself totally and irrevocably. This capacity is the possibility of love. Here again, no person or thing can compel this total gift of self. The entire finite realm, then, cannot fulfill our drive to totally receive and give, to share an infinite love.

Nevertheless, it is in and through the finite persons, things, and events interwoven into the fabric of our lives that we are drawn relentlessly to seek the infinite. Every choice or commitment we make, we make in view of the infinite. Our every decision and action embodies a stance toward the infinite. In all we meet we are looking for God. In all we choose we are opting for or against God. How is this concretely so?

In a negative way, we may try to make something finite into an infinite. We may try to find in bodily gratification, money, political influence, or the bond with another human being the sole answer to all our needs, the gratification of all our desires, the solution of all our problems. This in effect is idolatry. Sooner or later the finiteness of our idols shows through and leaves us emptier than ever. A marriage can follow this tragic path. At first one may avidly love the other as a magic answer to everything, but one is soon bitterly disappointed, angrily attacks and discards the partner, and lapses into a lonely hopelessness.

All our idols eventually crumble to dust. As they do so we may cling in desperation to the ashes. Or our disappointment may turn to anger, and we may curse their finiteness and lash out to destroy these gods that have failed. We may then collapse into a melancholic or defiant despair, thinking that our quest is in vain and that our pretension to infinity has trailed off into nothingness. This is atheism in its most negative sense.

In a more positive manner, though, we may choose what is finite but at the same time implicitly recognize both its finiteness and our own quest for something more. In this case we recognize the finite as something but not as everything. In choosing, we cherish its fragile value without clutching it, and if need be we let it go without lasting bitterness or hostility. We remain open to the infinite, seeing in the particular finite thing or person an expression of and a way to the infinite but not a substitute for it. A thing is a means to the infinite; a person shares our path.

Rather than making and breaking idols, we have in this case the sharing of "sacraments," encounters with persons and things that point our way to the infinite. Instead of falling into atheistic despair, we are sustained by a deeper hope which reaches beyond finite values without bypassing them. We come to trust that the silent infinity which surrounds us is indeed the ultimate reality and the source and goal of unconditional meaning. Where such a response emerges to an explicit level, it becomes adoration, total commitment in which a person falls into an awed silence.

The infinite is thus the mystery in the light of which we know any particular object and in view of which we make any particular choice. This mystery is like a circle which

envelopes our whole being. It is, so to speak, behind us as
that from which we reach. It is before us as that toward
which we reach. The experience of God can be seen as the
experience of this infinite mystery which at once asks and
answers the question which we are.

Let us further specify this experience and then bring
together our earlier considerations. This outreach, dis-
cerned in our inquiring mind and longing will, proceeds
from the heart or inmost core of our being. It is what is
deepest in us and indeed could be said to define us as
human persons: We are an outreach from the heart. All
our experiences willl reflect this character. They will
reflect both our inmost core and our furthest outreach.
These two poles are our points of contact with the infinite.
God may thus be depicted as the infinite mystery we touch
upon in our inmost core and in our furthest outreach. God
is that which is prior to our heart and further than our
outreach.

At the same time, our central orientation is present from
the beginning. It is given with our existence, not initiated
by us. Recall the example of the small child's efforts to explore and understand. This orientation arises from and is
sustained by the infinite toward which it is drawn. As finite
beings, too, we cannot grasp and contain the infinite. We
can only touch upon and be open to this "something more."
We may thus speak of what is deeper than our heart and
further than our outreach as source and goal, ground and
term, origin and end. In more personal language, we may refer
to this presence as enabler and summoner, giver and chal-
lenger, that elicits gratitude and responsibility. If we view
the human quest as a search for meaning, we may also speak
of a source and goal of the final meaningfulness of life.

A few important clarifications may be added here. The experience of God will be fullest at those times when we are most attuned to our inmost depths and furthest aspirations. These are the critical moments of life upon which Part Two will focus. They must be understood as occasions for discerning more clearly a presence which is always there, permeating our every experience. But we will not be discovering one object among other objects. If we look in this way, we will miss God—as if we were looking for our eyeglasses without realizing that we are looking through them. We discover God as the horizon in the light of which all is seen rather than as one item within that infinite horizon.

However, all our ideas and words apply directly only to the tangible things and persons within this horizon, not to the horizon itself. All our language about God falls short in this particular way. It never applies exactly, but only more or less. In more technical terms, we cannot speak of God univocally but only analogically. To think otherwise, to narrow God down to any concept of God, is to engage in a kind of mental idolatry. Our words will always falter. It will always be a little like using language about the stars to speak of the night sky, or that of trees and branches to talk of the light through which they are seen. Even when we speak of God as a person, we must be careful not to think too readily of God as one more person among others but rather as the mysterious source and goal of ourselves as persons.

Nevertheless, both our crucial encounters with the persons and things around us and our own inner life will profoundly affect how we conceive and express our awareness of the infinite mystery. God will be articulated as the

horizon and goal of *this* rather than *that* particular experience of our immense longing. I will portray God in one
instance as the betrayed toward whom I reach for forgiveness and healing. In another case I will think of God as the
presence to which I am grateful for the conviction of
meaning in my life. The various depth experiences are like
so many different fingers of an outstretched hand which
touch upon infinity at different points. The speech and
summons of the infinite to the mind and will of human
beings will also (to put it anthropomorphically) bear the
language and accent of the finite persons, cultures, and
environments through which it is mediated. So too will the
human response in word and action.

Finally, we may conclude with a few observations relating the above development to the Trinity and to the
traditionally called "theological virtues" of faith, hope, and
charity. The infinite mystery which we touch upon in our
inmost depths is the immanent Spirit. The infinite mystery
which we touch upon in our furthest outreach is the
transcendent Father. The infinite mystery which we touch
upon in the man Jesus is the incarnate Son. He is the true
analogue, the one word which fully expresses the infinite
mystery that eludes all our categories of thought and
speech.

In Jesus we learn that the infinity which surrounds our
being is not an endless sea of nothingness but a wellspring
of eternal life which enables and summons us to a fullness
of life even out of death. Jesus also utters his own version
of our initial question, "Where is your God?" He does so as
he tastes the bitter dregs of human finiteness and the
anguish of the human quest in the face of cruel death. He
utters it, not as an intellectual exercise but as a cry from the

depths: "My God, my God, why have you forsaken me?"
Yet he also gives voice to his total hope in and commitment
to the mystery when he says "Father, into your hands I
commend my spirit."

What of our response? The virtue of hope expresses the
underlying attitude of reaching out with trust into the
infinite mystery we call Father. When this attitude flows
into an outreach of our mind into the unfathomable,
beyond all we can directly comprehend, it becomes faith. In
its most explicit form it becomes acceptance of the Word of
truth embodied in Christ. When this attitude becomes an
outreach of our will into the uncontrollable, beyond all we
can directly manage, it becomes charity. Most explicitly, it
becomes acceptance of that infinite love dwelling within us
as Spirit.

That toward which we reach beyond all that we can
understand or control may be ultimately described in terms
of trustworthiness, truth, love. The infinite beyond all we
can comprehend is truth, uttered in the Word. The infinite
beyond all we can grasp and attain is love, bestowed in the
Spirit. So the infinite is totally trustworthy, is Father.

In the light of the perspective presented here in Part
One, we look now to specific pathways into the mystery we
call God.

# PART TWO

# Encounters

# CHAPTER FIVE

# Silence and Solitude

We have tried to unfold an approach to God as the infinite presence we encounter in our deepest human experience. We begin now to flesh out that vision by examining some specific experiences. These are pathways to our inmost core and furthest outreach, routes to a door opening to the infinite. They are points of contact with the mystery. Each such experience is like the finger of an outstretched hand: It does not grope toward nothingness but touches something ultimately real. Yet each finger touches infinity at a different place. By examining various outreaches and the depths from which they arise, we discover different specific avenues to that reality. Our experience of God may then become more vividly real to us, and our language more authentic and resonant. We start with the experience of silence in solitude.

God is the presence we encounter at the core of our being. But we are easily and often very far from that core. We readily skate along the periphery of our lives, going around in the circles of busyness, distraction, and noise, out of touch with our own self. But in the experience of silence in solitude we are drawn toward the center of our deepest self.

The road to silence is difficult to follow in a rushed and fevered age which surrounds itself with so much noise. Our own individual lives, too, are filled with many cares and duties which demand our attention and occupy our time. These daily activities, of course, can be a training ground where vague ideals are deflated by sharper insight and where self-preoccupation is pruned to allow the growth of patient, genuine caring. Our day, however, often seems to be comprised of a pile of unimportant activities that jostle and succeed one another in a random way. Our hearts lie hidden beneath the debris of a thousand trifles and are scattered in fragments among our piecemeal activities.

Pervading everything can be a ceaseless, nagging fear that each of us is utterly alone in a futile world. Perhaps we are all strangers caught up in a pointless tangle of empty hurryings to and fro. We might compare this scene to watching a television set with the volume turned off: The forced smiles, exaggerated gestures, frenzied dancing, and rapid-fire actions appear ludicrous. But if we keep the volume turned up high we may not notice the absurdity of it all. The flight from silence to noise in our age may be impelled by the dread that beneath the idle chatter lurks senseless chaos. It is as if we were shouting at life in a desperate attempt to win an argument. Perhaps we fear that if we are quiet we may hear the case that life makes for its own absurdity and be totally defeated. Again, it is as if we are running as fast as we can to hide from ourselves the fact that our course has no direction.

If we recognize that what we really seek cannot be found in all the clamor, we may have the courage to venture on occasion into silence. Then we may begin to find the inner self which we lost beneath the clutter or fled from in the din. We will now outline some of the steps on this journey into silence. In this discussion (as in those that follow) we are guided by, though by no means confined to, Karl Rahner's treatment of these topics.

We might select a lonely walk, a quiet church, or other private place where we will be undisturbed for a time. We must then summon up the resolve to be alone, to endure our own company. We must now turn our minds from the busy concerns of our daily affairs, quiet their lingering echoes, and gently set aside the preoccupations which make us anxious and tens. We should not then carry on a conversation with ourselves nor an imagined debate with others. This is not an occasion to reprove or to justify ourselves, either to ourselves or to an imagined audience. Such would not be interior silence, but a mere continuation of the noise, and it would remain on the surface level of the self.

Nor need we look for strange and exotic inner experiences; such things are peripheral. Above all, it is not a question of probing into ourselves as if we were objects under a microscope. Efforts to scrutinize ourselves from outside are self-defeating. They leave us as an outside observer, out of touch with our deepest self. Moreover, this can become an endless and sterile self-questioning in which we become imprisoned in the closed web of our own introspection. It is like stirring up the surface of a pond so that everything becomes murky, unclear—and, to continue the metaphor, creating a whirlpool in which we

drown. But if we let the surface become still, the depths of
the pond may become transparent.

What is required, then, is to stop, to wait, to listen
quietly. We must gradually empty ourselves of all else so as
to become open to the depths of our own being. We may, as
it were, let layer after layer of the outer self fall away. In this
way the inner core which these layers envelope can then lie
exposed to our awareness.

We may at first enjoy a kind of emotionally tinged
peacefulness. As we draw nearer and nearer to ourself,
however, we may recoil in horror at the conflicting urges,
the hollowness, the weakness, the betrayal that may rise to
the surface. We may come across the writhing coil of blind
forces and cravings unveiled by depth psychology. We may
find a barren and desolate wasteland bereft of life. Or it may
dawn upon us how really distant from us are all those with
whom we are supposedly bound by ties of love. At this
point the temptation is very strong to flee from such
unbearable awareness and return to the routine and distraction of everyday life.

If we do endure and bear with ourselves, we will discover
how everything that emerges in the stillness, and even our
very self, will appear as if encompassed and suffused by a
kind of indefinable emptiness and remoteness. It is like
being alone at night in a house filled with lights and
sounds—we notice these and nothing else. But if we
gradually shut off both lights and sounds, we will become
aware of the all-enveloping darkness of the night. In
silence, we may become aware that all our activities, our
very selves, and our whole finite world are, like that house,
contained within a silently surrounding infinity. In the
preceding chapter we tried to clarify intellectually this

infinite horizon. Here we are trying to point to it as a vivid experience.

What is involved is a striking sense of our own finiteness, felt not as an abstract idea nor as someone else's experience but as our very own reality. This is the stunning and possibly terrifying realization that I need not be, that I might not have been, that I may cease to be. If we do draw near to the center of our being, we will find a pinpoint of identity which appears to rest upon nothing and is suspended in the middle of nowhere. We may feel it as a distant and endless silence through which we are falling, or as a more oppressive silence and darkness which closes in upon us. At certain moments of anxiety it may seem that the bottom is falling out of our lives and indeed out of our very self. To profoundly experience such contingency is to realize that this is our permanent condition.

Is this all that the silence has to reveal? Is the surrounding infinity merely an empty abyss which eventually swallows us up? Is it merely a vast, empty background, a dark landscape against which all else is seen in its finite smallness and boundaries? Or is this surrounding infinity something more? Is a frightening sense of my own contingency the end of the journey into silence, or is it possible to go further?

If we persist in the silence and do not flee in terror back to the surface of our lives, the ambiguity may be resolved. However, no voice will pierce the silence. No separate word will enter the silence from outside and speak to us. To look for or expect such a word is to seek again an item or object within the horizon while missing the horizon itself. It is to wait in vain for an idol.

In this context we might rather say that the silence itself

speaks. Any word that comes is a word that comes *not into* but *out of* the silence. And the word that comes out of the infinite silence is . . . ourself. We may in the darkness come to experience ourself as word, as a someone uttered from the silence. What does this mean? It means that as we get in touch with the depth of our being we may, without losing our sense of contingency, come to experience ourselves as beings gifted with meaning and purpose.

Once we realize to any degree that we are neither self-originated nor necessary, there are only two ways of understanding ourself: either as fluke or as gift. Either we are like driftwood cast up randomly and without reason on the brief shore of our life, only to be swallowed up all too soon in a churning sea of chaos, or we are like a precious carving which reflects order and design. If we are contingent, we are not self-originating but the expression of something else. If we are absurd and pointless, then we reflect a blind and aimless process, devoid of intelligence and will. If we do have meaning and purpose, if we do make sense and have a destiny, we reflect a source which may be analogously described in terms of consciousness and freedom. We are gift. It is out of this all-encompassing silence that we flow as gift.

The analogy of the word, and of word out of silence, is helpful here. Earlier we noted that in personal sharing one freely takes something of oneself, embodies it in a word, and offers it to another. One's word is a conscious symbol of self-giving. It expresses one's understanding and caring. If I silently arrive at the core of my contingent being and experience myself as gift, then I too am an expression of understanding and caring. I am somehow known and loved at my very core. I am not a mere nonsense syllable or random sound. I am a word, uttered with meaning and love from the infinite silence.

We must be careful here not to reduce the mystery to a too-anthropomorphic reality. We are still speaking of the limitless context within which we are contained. This infinite horizon remains silent and dark. No word comes to us from without to break the silence. Yet we may experience ourselves as gift, as word, as expression of knowledge and love. Then we may say that the best perspective from which to view ourselves and the most fitting way to describe the infinite horizon is in these terms. I do not directly see the infinite, but I do experience myself in the light of infinite meaning and in view of infinite purpose.

In the recesses of silence, therefore, we do not experience a separate being in addition to ourselves. Rather we may experience ourselves as utterance and gift. In this case, that from which flows our very self as gift and word is what is meant by the term "God." God is the ineffable, unfathomable silence in which we are contained and from which we are uttered as word of meaning and love. The point of contact is our inmost self, unveiled not in noise or introspection but in deep interior silence.

This experience is articulated in the doctrine of creation. The first chapter of Genesis portrays creation as a word of God which draws order out of chaos and brings forth what is good. Order and goodness constitute the basic character of all that exists. All that exists is a word expressive of understanding and love.

In this regard, belief in creation or in a creator God need not be interpreted as asserting that there is a naively viewed outside supreme being who has manufactured everything. To believe in creation is to experience profoundly the order and goodness of which Genesis speaks and to acknowledge, at least implicitly, its source. More specifically, it is to experience gratefully oneself and others as gift or word and to strive to live according to the significance and value implied therein. Such faith entails accepting the self that is given to us, not as mere driftwood nor even as a finished product but as living raw material, sacred yet incomplete. We then attempt to fashion that material into a lasting work of art. (We will speak more of this aspect in the next chapter when dealing with freedom and responsibility.)

Moreover, if the infinite silence is uttered in us as word and gift, understanding and caring, order and goodness, this silence is best regarded as source of truth and love. Our earlier comments on the Trinity come to mind. Jesus is the truthful Word of God. Spirit is the Love of God. What is bestowed or bestows itself in Word and Spirit is called Father. The Father is the infinite Silence who speaks himself completely in the Word, Jesus, and enters and remains present in the human heart as indwelling Spirit.

We are each a word of God. Rather, that of which we are a word is what is meant by "God." For the Christian, however, it is in the person, works, life, death, and resurrection of Jesus that we find the most complete word. He most fully gives voice to the eternal silence.

Christ is not only Word out of silence. He not only comes from the Father; he also continually voices his thanks and commitment to the Father. The experience of self as word and gift also evokes gratitude and adoration.

It is possible to arrive at a profound conviction of the gifted sacredness of oneself and the meaningfulness of one's life. A person may do so despite his or her limitedness and non-necessity and even despite the brokenness and wrongness within self and world. For this conviction, one is grateful. This gratitude need not be explicitly thought of or stated. Nor is it just an emotion which comes and goes sporadically. It is more like a tone or undertone which pervades one's entire life.

This is true of any deeply rooted conviction. It is more than just an unexamined thought, inherited opinion, cultural view, or stubborn prejudice. It springs from an insight whose unquestionable truth dawns upon us with a clarity and force which may disturb and challenge us. In such situations we are not pulled toward an arrogant self-righteousness or disdain for others. Rather, we are humbled and thankful for what we have seen or realized. If we desire to share that vision with others it is not because it is ours. It is because it is true, truer even than we are. It is not as though we have grasped, but as though we have been grasped by something.

If we are really able to speak that truth or, in the case of music and art, to play or paint what is truly beautiful, it is not as though we ourselves have done so. It is as though something has been spoken or played or painted through us. Without our thinking about it, we have all the while been more fully present and more fully ourselves than ever before. In a more complete sense, we have become word of God. The infinite silence echoes with more exquisite clarity through us, and the infinite darkness becomes more radiantly transparent. When this occurs, there is a sense of having been blessed.

Such is eminently the case with the conviction of the meaning and worth of human life. This conviction cannot be put on or shed like an outer garment. It resides in the marrow of one's bones, arising out of lived experience. It is a gift for which one bears responsibility and which can be preserved only by cultivating it in silence and by sharing it quietly with others. Some persons do not see themselves and their lives as a precious gift but as a cruel jest or a thankless burden. One who sees life as a worthwhile gift will not be eager to condemn those who view it in that negative way. Rather, such a person may react as Jesus did when he wept over the people of Jerusalem who could not accept his peace-giving message (Luke 19:41-44)— saddened that something so true is not seen, that something so valuable is not received.

A gratitude which tends to permeate one's life and issue into responsibility and sharing flows from the profound experience of self as word and gift. Again, the one to whom we are ultimately grateful and before whom we are called to responsibility and generosity is what is meant by "God."

At the same time, this gratitude cannot be separated from a sense of contingency. If we are gift, we need not have been given. The finite gift that we are is always seen in the light of the infinite. The fragile house of our finiteness is ever outlined against the night of infinity. At this stage of the silent journey to the center we are struck with wonder and awe at the immensity of the silence and darkness. We are completely overwhelmed by the total otherness or transcendence of the infinite mystery. Gratitude gives rise to adoration, the stuttering expression of this overwhelming awe.

The infinite is both the goal in view of which all is chosen and the light in which all is seen. Our human quest for something more searches for an infinity which fills the expanse of our will and evokes our total response and commitment. This is actually a reaching out for something which so overwhelms us as to drive us to our knees. We seek an infinite to worship and adore. Through the doorway to infinity at the core of our being we may glimpse enough to be impelled to adoring commitment.

This experience of awe may well lie behind and form the basis of the biblical stories of theophanies, or manifestations of the sacred. Something of a force or power which pulsates through the universe may also be sensed (at times in an altogether eerie fashion) in certain places human beings have regarded as especially sacred. In the ruins of a Mayan temple or in those of a World War II concentration camp one may perceive a summons to silence.

Adoration is not flattery. It is not a kind of superficial fawning directed to a whimsical and occasionally cruel despot in order to assure his good graces or twist his arm in one's own favor. Adoration is rather the connatural response to the experience of being overwhelmed by the transcendent otherness of the infinite.

Nevertheless, total otherness cannot be divorced from total nearness, nor the experience of contingency from that of gift. The point of contact with the infinite otherness is my own inmost self experienced as gift which is somehow known and loved. Transcendence and immanence belong together. The prophet Isaiah, for example, speaks of Yahweh as the Holy One of Israel. As the Holy One, Yahweh is utterly distinct from all that is finite and sinful, from all that contains nothingness or wrongness. Yet Yahweh is precisely the Holy One *of Israel,* totally near and turned toward Israel.

The Gospel story of the Transfiguration similarly portrays this Holy One as fully present in the man Jesus. In Jesus, immanence and transcendence become incarnate, are given flesh and voice. Jesus is the Spirit-filled Son of the Father. To put it differently: In the core of our being we discover a presence which is totally other and is embodied in the man Jesus. We discover the Spirit of the Father who is uttered in Christ. We are enabled and summoned to gratitude for nearness and to adoration before otherness.

To take the gift and the word that we are and say "Father" into the infinite darkness and silence is not merely to give voice to a sentimental feeling of endearment. In its truest sense it is a cry wrung out of the depth of the heart, in joy or in anxiety, uttered by one who is overwhelmed at once by the total otherness of God and by the total trustworthiness and nearness of God. This word of ours then becomes a prelude to the silence of adoration, in which the human person falls speechless before the ineffable mystery.

# CHAPTER SIX

# Freedom and Responsibility

The self which in quiet solitude opens onto the silence of God is a free and responsible self. We are free insofar as our self is placed into our own hands. How we accept and fashion that self depends considerably upon us. It is our responsibility. We are also questing beings, filled with an immense longing. We are drawn to take the self we must shape and to give it to something worthwhile and fulfilling. This commitment is also our responsibility. Put differently, the word which we are is given to ourselves to speak, and we are drawn to utter it completely. The gift which we are is first offered to ourselves, and we long to bestow it completely.

What might this experience suggest? In our approach, the infinite reality from which our self flows as free and responsible and toward which we are summoned to entrust and commit our entire self is what is meant by "God." In the experience of freedom, God is what we touch upon as freedom's source and goal, its enabler and summons.

The voice of silence is also the voice of conscience. We will now explore more closely this experience of freedom and responsibility.

"Freedom" may seem to denote only a hollow slogan devoid of real content. As suggested earlier, we are, whether we will it or not, surrounded and pushed by constant noise, incessant demands, and inducements from many quarters. We are afflicted by competing urges within us, and beneath them seethe even more primordial forces. We may also feel small and helpless before the massiveness of our society and its institutions, public and private. As a result it is easy to see freedom as just a small corner of our life where we can escape from the pressures and do what we wish. Even our wishes may be reduced to passing and ever-changing surface impulses, far removed from deeper needs and wants. As our life trickles away we may hunt for a scape-goat for the gnawing dissatisfaction which will not let us go. We may blame society or our background or else turn upon ourselves as of little worth.

Inherent in our discontent is a craving for a fuller life. We want to understand and to have a say in what is happening in our own life. We prefer to be the author rather than the victim or the bystander of our own life story. If we have indeed been gifted with meaning and purpose we must also be summoned to know that meaning and to freely achieve that purpose. To be fully alive is to be fully aware, free, and responsibly committed. Is this a possibility, or an illusion? If it is a possibility we may think of God as that which enables and calls us to a fullness of life, awareness, freedom and commitment, even out of the many forms of deadness, ignorance, slavery, and indiffer-

ence which beset us. We will attempt to depict this process
and the experience of God it contains.

As our lives begin they are largely in the hands of others.
Only gradually does our unique self emerge and come into
our own hands. As a flower grows out of its roots and soil,
so our freedom only slowly unfolds from a context which
both supports and limits it. A human being is a child of the
physical universe. Our chemical content, bodiliness, sensi-
bility, sexuality, and passage from birth to death link us to
the world of matter and biological life. As members of the
specifically human family we have a higher degree both of
interiority and of openness to what is other than ourselves.
Our capacity for self-awareness and for relationship, and
our orientation to the infinite distinguish us from other life
forms. We dwell within a particular social and cultural
milieu, endowed with its own customs and conventions,
mentality and public opinion, and coercive pressures. We
also receive a certain kind of family upbringing, in which
security, challenge, love, and trust are present or absent in
varying degrees.

We thus begin and develop within a familial, social,
cultural, human, biological, and physical context. The gift
which we are is given within this total environment, not in
isolation. The setting is like the language in which the
word that we are is spoken. Within this setting emerges a
human nature, already moulded and channeled in a particular way, and a unique person to which it belongs.

Our human nature includes all the capacities, tendencies, needs, and situations which necessarily belong to the
human condition. These elements both define our possibilities and set our limits. The age in which we live also

confers a distinct stamp and coloring upon them. They are further developed or stifled, directed and configured, by the conditioning factors studied in the social sciences.

We may at times become more acutely aware of these elements which shape our existence. It may strike us, for example, how we still react in many situations according to patterns ingrained long ago, even though these patterns are harmful. The inert grip of our past weighs heavily upon us. Unresolved inner conflicts continue to exhaust us and to nourish hostility toward others. On the other hand, we may know that we continue to draw insight from an early episode in our life and that another's concern for us as a child is an enduring source of strength.

Our essential human characteristics, as nurtured or marred by our surroundings, are like many different layers around the central core of the person to whom they belong. At that inmost core a person is himself or herself and no other. He or she is a distinct self which has never been before, a radically unique spiritual center of which there is no carbon copy. All the enveloping layers of our concrete human makeup are the outer dimensions of this personal center. Through them we also make contact with our environing world and receive its influences. Each distinct person is like a stone dropped into a pond, whose emanating circles overlap and flow into those of others.

There are occasions when one's radical uniqueness is more forcibly felt. We instinctively sense an injustice when we are stereotyped, whether by race, ethnic group, or social position. We may feel our uniqueness at a time when we are extremely lonely and find no one with whom we can simply be ourselves without defence or reserve, no one who can truly hear us without having to categorize, judge, or give advice. At other times we are gripped by a need for solitude in order to become attuned to our own center. We realize also the burden and promise of an important decision facing us—one which no other can make for us. And we grieve at the loss or death of someone very close to us because we recognize that this person can never be replaced.

Our freedom is most truly situated at this unique personal core. Our concrete human makeup is like the raw material with which the core person must work. It is raw material that is blemished and scarred in some ways, yet possessed of a rough, partially hidden beauty. This material needs to be carved out, refined, and released. The core person is like a sculptor who must take it and, while respecting its basic properties, shape it by his or her free decision.

Only gradually does our whole self come into our hands. Only over a long period of time does our humanness come to be at the disposal of our personhood. As we slowly move from childhood to maturity, the many dimensions of our raw material enter into our awareness and thereby fall within the scope of our freedom and responsibility. At the outset a little boy, let us say, is almost totally immersed in his environment. As he gradually distinguishes himself from his family he becomes more and more aware of himself as a separate person. He then asserts himself over against his family, usually by stubbornness and frequent use of the word "no." Yet this separation occasions anxiety, and the child repeatedly seeks reassurance of his family's presence and of his own belonging.

As this example tries to show, the growth in self-awareness and freedom is a process of differentiating

oneself from what is other than self and then assuming a
more conscious and deliberate stance toward that other.
We distance ourselves from and take up an attitude toward
our family, school, society, and the like. We step back from
the other persons and things of our environment and then
deliberately relate ourselves to them. Our response can be
one of flight, refusal, or hostility. It can be one of openness,
welcome, or self-giving. Or it may blend all of these in
varying degrees.

We may finally come to differentiate our whole self from
all that is and take up a stance toward reality, life, existence
itself. The culmination occurs when we explicitly differentiate ourselves and all that is finite from its infinite context.
We come to think consciously of ourselves as finite and
other than the infinite. We take up a deliberate stance
toward the infinite. We regard the mystery either as void or
as ultimate reality. We are grateful or resentful. We refuse,
or we commit ourselves. We say either "I will not serve" or
"Into your hands I commend my spirit."

It was previously emphasized that a background awareness of and orientation to the infinite underlies all our
knowing and choosing. In the situation just mentioned, the
knowing becomes fully conscious and the choosing quite
specific. Yet each of our conscious decisions does embody
an implicit stand toward the infinite. In all we freely do we
utter a yes or no to the mystery of God. This constitutes our
fundamental responsibility.

We will now consider more implicit aspects of the
experience of God that are contained in the experience of
personal responsibility. We are able to experience ourself as
gift rather than fluke. This gift, we may add, flows from its
source through the somewhat crooked streams of our total

environment. It also flows into our very uniqueness. If I am gift, I am so as a human being and as this particular person. I am gift in my very uniqueness and am therefore somehow known and loved in my very singularity. As who and what I am comes into my hands, I am called to an acceptance and response that is irreplaceably my own. I am endowed with a responsibility that is inescapable and personal. In brief, I am somehow uttered and summoned *by name.* The source and term of this unique gift and call is what is meant by "God."

The uniqueness of this gift and call is a possible interpretation of biblical stories of vocation, such as those of Abraham and Paul. Both men are said to receive a call by name from God. Whatever the factual circumstances may have been, each profoundly experienced himself as personally addressed and given a specific vocation. This path was his alone to follow and was decisive for others as well as for himself. Both men are given a new name. This change brings out the uniqueness of the call and the transformation it evokes or expresses in the person. "God" is the name for the ineffable source and summons encountered in this experience.

As a new or deeper aspect of our self and of our situation comes to the fore, we must inevitably deal with it. We must decide about it, in attitude if not in action. A first and most obvious area of responsibility lies in the making of decisions.

We do make countless decisions in our daily lives. Many of them, such as details of diet or hygiene, are done out of habit or routine. Many concern trivial matters to which we give scant attention; they merely glance off the surface of our character. Other choices—such as those concerning a

career, marriage, or emigration—draw upon all the re-
sources of our past and shape the whole course of our
future. There are also more hidden moments which nonetheless strike a person as a crossroads in his or her life. A
trail of moral compromises must either be stopped or
pursued completely. A sensitivity to spiritual issues must
be cultivated now or else virtually snuffed out. Doubts
about the direction of one's life are heeded or dismissed
altogether. A final choice between loyalty or betrayal of a
friend is demanded. One either listens to one's children
now or severs the last link of communication. A relationship is either awakened or left to die behind barricades of
monotony and mistrust. A stand must be taken today on a
vital social issue, or the opportunity is lost forever.

At such moments we experience our responsibility as
personal and inescapable. No other can make this decision
for us. It concerns our very self and is ours alone to make.
We cannot flee such choices any more than we can run
away from ourselves. We may try to evade the responsibility by simply drifting through life, by letting circumstances and other persons make our decisions for us. But
the drifting is still our own decision, for which we are as
responsible as we are for any other decision.

We sense the cruciality of such times of decision. They
are pivotal points at which our life in its entirety comes into
play and its fulfillment or failure is weighed in the balance.
Our very identity appears to be at stake in the decision to be
made. We may struggle and agonize over that decision, and
venture into it with fear and anxiety, for the stakes are
high, the cost great, and the direction sometimes obscure.
At other times we may act with sureness and confidence
because the right path seems so clear.

We may claim, of course, that our decisions by and large do not matter, because in so many instances we cannot implement them in practice or because they make no appreciable impact on any individual or on society. However, a fundamental dimension of freedom is involved in our inner attitudes, and specifically in our response to what is unalterable in our lives, whether the unalterable is rooted in outward circumstances or in the human condition itself. The human condition includes not only our longing for "something more" but also the suffering which accompanies our existence and the death which ends it. The way we deal with these realities (which we will treat later) profoundly affects the shape and direction of our lives.

Beneath the assertion that our decisions do not matter may lurk the suspicion that *nothing* we think or say or do really matters. We are then in fact affirming that we ourselves do not matter and that our lives have no significance. To the extent that such an attitude is free, it is a fundamental option in the direction of despair. Conversely, if we are convinced that our decision is vital, we are implying that our lives are meaningful or at least can become so. For it is through such decisions that we forge our lives and our selves. We are in that case presupposing a basis of meaning and hope.

If it is crucial to choose, it is just as crucial to choose rightly. When we discern that a given action is here and now demanded by our conscience, we experience that demand as unconditional. To decide this way and not that way is not arbitrary; it must be done as a matter of life and death. Only then will we be true to ourselves and not betray our own inmost truth. The decision which stands before us also has an unconditional value. It does not immediately pass into oblivion, as if it had never been made; otherwise it could not be so important. It has a significance which somehow endures.

A person gives the most striking witness to the unconditional character of such decisions when he or she refuses to forsake convictions or betray a friend even in the face of death. This fidelity implies that one's truth and love become such a part of one's very identity that to abandon them would be to destroy one's true self. It would be a deeper form of death. Such a commitment is also presumed to have a validity which even physical death cannot negate. It is felt to be in some way deeper, stronger, and more enduring than physical death itself. A moral decision, therefore, on which we stake ourselves and our life is experienced as placing an unconditional demand and having an unconditional validity.

How do we determine which decisions are good and which are evil? No attempt will be made here to enter the complex arena of moral principles and decision-making. But we will briefly reflect on the metaphor of the person as sculptor shaping the raw material of his or her humanity. A sculptor must respect and work along with, not against, the material he or she is shaping. In shaping our self, we must respect the basic structures of our humanity. We should discover and follow the grain of what is truly human. We must do nothing which dehumanizes self or others. We must also regard as sacred and treat accordingly the unique personal centers to which that humanity belongs. We need to modify our social context more in the direction of cherishing rather than violating what is authentically human and personal. Lastly, we should recognize both our finiteness and our infinite longing. We must not idolatrously make of ourselves or another something infinite but must instead foster an underlying openness to the truly infinite mystery.

In summary, we experience an inescapable, personal, crucial, and unconditional responsibility for our decisions, especially the key decisions of our lives. In doing so, we experience also the reason why there is such responsibility. The ultimate ground of human responsibility is what is meant by "God."

In experiencing responsibility for our decisions we also experience ourselves as gift, gradually given into our own conscious and free hands. We sense a uniquely personal call and unconditional demand, addressed to each of us by name. This call summons us to make vital decisions consonant with our own and others' sacredness and thereby to carve out a life of enduring meaning and hope. The initial source from which we flow as gift to ourselves, the ultimate ground in which we are rooted as inescapably responsible, and the final horizon before which we stand accountable—this is what is meant by "God."

To put it more concretely, the silence onto which the center of our being opens is a listening silence. We experience our decision as heard, weighed, and judged. It is as though our life were lived out upon a stage whose footlights were brightly lit. We see only the stage itself and beyond it nothing but darkness. Our life is performed before that darkness in which a presence is felt. In the experience of responsibility we sense the unseen presence before which we are finally accountable. And that is what is meant by "God."

As a further step we may now examine how responsible

freedom concerns not only individual decisions but the very shaping and gift of our whole self. At first glance, freedom may appear to be the capacity to make a series of arbitrary and unconnected choices which can always be reversed. Our journey through life, in this view, resembles a walk through a supermarket in which we randomly select this item or that, with the freedom to return any item before passing through the final check-out. In this perspective, our lives become a row of fragments set side by side, or loose beads without a thread. There is nothing to hold them together. Moreover, if all our decisions could be endlessly revised, none would really matter. Each would be a disposable item in a throwaway life.

We are most acutely aware of our responsibility precisely in those decisions in which our whole self is involved and the future course of our life is at stake. Through our key decisions we do not just decide what to do; we determine who we are and who we will become. Hence our freedom most basically concerns our very self and the tenor of our life as a whole. Our individual choices are linked together insofar as they express and help to fashion our total identity.

In addition, the more deeply centered and comprehensive a decision, the less it is subject to revision. For the most part it is quite easy to reverse a decision to read a newspaper or to have dinner a half hour later. But we do not readily change our deepest convictions or set aside our closest bonds. In such cases it is more accurate to speak of commitment or fundamental option than of choice in a more restricted sense.

By way of illustration, when one person pledges to love another "forever," he or she is not specifying a certain amount of time. If the word "forever" is changed into an estimated number of years according to one's statistical life expectancy, its whole meaning is lost. If the commitment is genuine and not illusory, something quite different is intended. The individual is saying that his or her promise to the other is without limits or conditions and that it will not be reversed. One is really affirming that who one is, and how one freely defines oneself includes being for the other without reserve.

Our deepest commitments are unconditional and final. They become part of our total self. Through them we define who we are. Freedom in its fullest sense is the possibility of and responsibility for such commitment. To be free is to be capable of and liable for the total and irrevocable gift of self from the heart. It is the capacity to write our own definition of who we are. We write this definition with our life. We gradually put our whole self freely yet finally into an action or series of actions, a pattern and direction of life, which shapes and expresses who we are.

There is indeed a deep longing within us to gather and give our whole self from the heart. This is the same restless yearning for the infinite "something more," beyond all we immediately encounter. From the present angle it may be viewed as a longing for something to which we can give ourselves completely without being disappointed again.

Certainly our world is a continual flux of physical, biological, and social forces which seem never-ending in their complexity and diversity. Our own makeup contains a whole range of capacities and drives, often in conflict with one another. Our lives are comprised of many and varied activities, all too often of a trivial kind. Nevertheless we have a deep-seated wish to gather up all this multiplicity into the intense pursuit of one all-embracing goal, worthy of all the toil and devotion of the human heart. We seek a oneness which weaves together these many strands into something of beauty.

We may settle for the hollow unity of having a "one-track mind" or being a "one-dimensional person." We simply shut out, by inattention, neglect, or force, what we cannot incorporate, or else we try to make something finite our one exclusive goal. Our real quest, however, is for a wholeness in which are gathered and pieced together and healed all the scattered fragments of our life. We seek a full oneness which reconciles and goes beyond all the contradictions and polarities of our everyday life. To use the image of Isaiah, we seek a land where the wolf and the lamb feed together (Isaiah 65:25).

Thus the question our longing freedom contains is this: What, if anything, is worth the gift of one's whole self? To what or to whom can a person confide all that he or she has and is? Where is one to find the pearl of great price, the hidden treasure, the one thing necessary which will not scatter, disperse, break apart, or leave us empty but will gather, reconcile, heal, make whole, and complete us?

To experience ourselves as enabled and summoned to reach out and trustingly confide ourselves to this ultimate unseen unity is to touch what is meant by "God." God is the all-encompassing, healing, and fulfilling oneness which evokes the total gift of self. God is the ultimate goodness which underlies and integrates all values. The acute experience of this underlying oneness which pervades all that is, yet transcends all that is, is what the mystical writers describe as the goal of contemplative prayer.

The doctrine of the Trinity expresses something similar. That within us which enables us to gather and give ourselves is the Spirit. That beyond us which summons us to this total commitment is the Father. That incarnate model according to which we are to shape ourselves is the man Jesus. The doctrine of the Trinity points to a oneness which is fullness. Christian monotheism is not the bare abstract assertion that there is only one God. It is not the proclamation of a monolithic "onliness." The trinitarian focus suggests an ultimate oneness which includes, gathers, and transcends everything. This is an all-embracing unity from which everything flows as from its originating source and to which everything is called to return as to its all-integrating goal.

In sum, the infinite silence from which we are uttered as a uniquely meaningful word is a listening silence, overhearing the decisions of our heart. It is likewise a beckoning silence which calls forth the total gift of ourselves. Our self is given in a precious but unfinished state, with the summons to fashion it into a lasting work of art. We do so by gathering and giving that self from the heart into the infinite mystery, at least implicitly. Now, it is preeminently through other persons that we receive the call and respond to it. This encounter with God through other persons is the topic of our next chapter.

# CHAPTER SEVEN

# Love

The self gradually given into our own hands is a precious gift which comes to us through the hands of others. We shape and give direction to that self with and before others, whose own worth we are summoned to respect. In experiencing the preciousness of the self that is given to us and the challenge to respond to the worth of others, we touch upon their mysterious source. In terms of our approach in this book, the infinite mystery from which we flow as valuable and which calls us to respond to the worth of others is what is meant by "God." In the experience of being valued and of acknowledging the value of another, we touch upon God. In short, we discover God in receiving and giving love. Let us further explore this matter.

To make a gift to another person, especially the gift of oneself, is to recognize a value in that person. We imply that he or she is worth our time, attention, effort, the sharing of our inner life. He or she is worthy of our consideration and care. To say that we may experience

ourself as gift rather than fluke is also to imply that we are
somehow valued. In this case the valuing is not partial,
mixed with illusion, or conditional. Rather, it is the real,
total, unique self that is valued, for this is the gift conferred. The worth is not presumed but is bestowed along
with the self and is therefore inseparable from it. To be a
human person is already to be valuable. Before we decide or
act we are already valuable. There is a worth without
conditions which simply goes with being a human person.
The ultimate source from which we flow is a valuing
source.

We are not assuming that everyone experiences life in
this way, nor are we lapsing into a naive anthropomor-
phism. It is not a matter of saying that life is precious and
that therefore there is a God. Rather, in our experience of a
human being, whether oneself or another, it is possible to
discern an unconditional worth. We discern it as there
from the beginning, independently of ourselves, and in a
being which is finite and contingent. We therefore discover
it as gift. In doing so, we touch upon the source of that gift.
This source is what is meant by "God."

The gift and the call enshrined in human sacredness
echo through our environment. We gradually grow in
awareness and responsible freedom by emerging from and
relating to our overall milieu, which at once nurtures and
mars us in various ways. This environment is most essentially one of persons. It includes chiefly the people we live
and associate with, whose lives more directly interact with
our own. This interaction reaches beyond the interpersonal sphere to larger social groups and today extends in
some degree to the entire human community. Thus the
divine gift and call may be said to speak through the

self-giving of others to us and through the claim that others' worth places upon our conscience.

In a first and most obvious way, the gift which we are comes through conception and birth. It comes through our parents and others who look after us in our early years. Here a person is first valued or disvalued, is pushed toward regarding himself or herself as gift or as fluke.

We spoke earlier of children's desire to be told of their origins in a story which reassures them that they are worthwhile and that they belong. It is significant, too, that stories about religious figures, such as Moses and Jesus, often give prominence to their birth. The same is true of many folktale figures, such as Sleeping Beauty and Snow White. Religious stories and folktales like these have a certain magical quality. They tell of a birth that is special— and so of a person who is special. The birth is the result of a promise. And so the child who is born is always a gift and never just the product of the parents. In traditional religious language, the child is referred to as a gift from God.

These stories express a conviction far stronger than any pious sentimentality. From the very beginning, they hold, the child is a distinct person who is not just an offshoot, possession, or reflection of the parents but is also a gift to them. By the child's very presence, he or she is a gift of special value to be welcomed with gratitude and cherished with respect. If the infinite mystery is indeed a source which founds and respects our value, then it is by being valued that we are told the truth about this mystery and about ourselves. By intelligently and freely caring for their daughter or son, parents do embody and convey this truth to the child.

Truth is something experienced and lived, not merely thought and talked about. Truth is told by actions, not just by words. To the extent that any human being is treated with dignity, he or she is told the truth. It is a profound tragedy of human existence that those who are told soon and often that they are of no value tend to believe and live this account and to retell it to others. All too readily our lives can become less a word of quiet caring than a cry of pain and anger. Perhaps the degree of violence in a society inversely reflects the degree to which its members esteem themselves and others.

If our worth is a gift conferred with our very existence and identity, it is intrinsic and enduring. It may be ignored, denied, or violated, but it cannot be taken away. Parents convey to the child a sense of this intrinsic and enduring value when their cherishing is not haphazard or intermittent but consistent and stable. By being continually valued, no matter what, we learn to believe in our own enduring worth. In our youngest days we are dependent upon others, physically, mentally, emotionally—in every area. We can only be open to receive. We have to trust. If this trust is not betrayed but is met by a constant and trustworthy love, we are told the truth. The finite environment reflects the ultimate context.

This view is far removed from the concept of God as a kind of super-parent who watches over us. To the child, reality means most immediately and directly his or her parents. It is in the experience of the family that the child first comes to form judgments and attitudes about life. If there is worth and meaning to human life, we will more readily discover that truth in a setting which supports and evokes our trust, not in one which features distrust and the defensiveness and aggression which follow in its wake. We are not advocating shielding the child from all harshness. Rather, we must try to provide a framework within which he or she may deal with the hurtful and destructive elements of life without being devoured by them or without seeing in them the essence of life.

Speaking of God as Father does not mean projecting into the heavens the image of an all-powerful parent. Instead, it affirms that in the experience of trustworthiness we touch the final truth. We encounter a source which grounds unalterably our intrinsic worth, and so we may describe this source as trustworthy, faithful, immutable—as Father. In this light we may perhaps best understand the Gospel lesson about becoming as little children—maintaining an attitude of basic trust and openness, in all circumstances of life, despite experiences which seem to invite us to close ourselves and hide behind walls of fear and hostility.

We spoke earlier of God as ground and term of the experience of meaning. A sense of intrinsic worth and a sense of meaning go together. If our life has importance, so have we who live it. If we are worthless, so are our lives. A person who seriously considers or attempts suicide frequently cites as reason that he or she is no good and nobody cares. On the other hand, if someone does care, one is good, and life is worth living. Another's love fosters a trust in the meaningfulness of life. In this way, too, the experience of being valued puts us in touch with what is meant by "God." Again, we may reflect upon how best to interpret this experience. We need not conclude somewhat abstractly from our deep sense of worth and meaning that there is a God whom we already picture in a certain way and situate, so to speak, outside this experience. Rather, our lives may resonate with a deep sense of gratitude to a hidden source. We may not explicitly think of this source or have a name for it, but the gratitude that pervades our life is nonetheless very real. And the word "God" may come to designate the one to whom our thanks reaches out.

Love is a gift of self to another who is valued. Until now we have focused chiefly upon the receiving side, the experience of being valued. This must be present before we ourselves can give, because we can only make a gift of ourselves to the extent that we value ourselves. Otherwise we will believe that we have nothing to offer and that no one would need or want us.

In presenting a gift we usually wrap it in a neat and colorful package. We want the gift itself, which is more valuable, to be a surprise discovered in an appropriate setting. When we present our very self to another we wrap it, so to speak, in our presence, words, and actions. If we regard ourselves as of little or no worth we will not make the offer. We will try to hide beneath the wrapping— that is, to conceal ourselves beneath externals and avoid discovery.

Our hunger for the infinite and for a total meaningfulness includes a longing to be of lasting value ourselves. That is why the feeling of utter worthlessness is so excruciatingly painful. The repeated use of alcohol to the point of "feeling no pain," along with other gradual and more direct forms of self-destruction, may well be an attempt to put an end to the pain of living without a sense of worth. Without a basic self-esteem and self-acceptance our life tends to become an unending effort or even a compulsive, frantic, desperate struggle to prove a value in which we do not believe.

Relationships with others reflect this predicament. We tend to view others as either needs or threats. We either cling to them or dominate them in order to boost our own faltering self-image, or else we flee from them as undermining forces. We are driven, not free, and on that account also we cannot love.

Only if we become convinced of our intrinsic value, present from the beginning as gift, which we neither can nor need to prove, do we experience a truth which sets us free. Only then are we delivered from preoccupation with our own emptiness; only then can we accept ourselves, see others as they concretely are, and respond to their essential value. We are then able to realize that we have and are something to offer and that others are worthy of this gift. And we implicitly acknowledge the source and respond to the summons with generosity, whether or not we use the word "God."

We must beware of oversimplification. The alternatives are not either sheer acceptance or sheer rejection of self and others. Most of us struggle between these two poles and the attitudes and behavior to which they give rise. The issue is further complicated by the realities of death and sin, which we have yet to consider. Nor are we totally determined by past influences to which we can shift all responsibility. From those who have shaped us we have probably received both gifts and wounds. We are challenged to grow beyond resentment and hostility by becoming grateful for the gifts and forgiving the wounds. In coming to grips with all these matters, positive convictions take firmer root in a nuanced and realistic way.

These reflections shed some light on the Christian concept of God as love. When we love another, we put our very self into the word or action which we share. In encountering that word or action, the other truly encounters us as we are instead of meeting with a disguise or deceit. To say that each one of us is a word of God means that we truly reflect our infinite source. Our deepest longings, therefore, do not deceive us. They are not vain illusions, but put us in touch with truth. Our longing for worth does not lie to us. It puts us in touch with an infinite source of value, and this we call "God."

The unconditional worth we have been considering belongs to every person. Everyone we meet or even affect indirectly has, therefore, a claim to our respect. The experience of this worth in self and others and its claim upon us is the root moral experience. It provides the ground of all other moral values, principles, or rules. These are nothing other than attempts to spell out, in general or in specific circumstances, what heeds or violates that worth. Within this human claim, as we will see, echoes the divine claim summoning our total response.

The degree and kind of claim does, of course, vary tremendously with the situation. It may entail a simple politeness or an intimate conversation. What is called for certainly cannot be reduced to a vague attitude of being superficially and harmlessly "nice" to everyone we come across. It can involve uttering unwelcome truths, challenging and demanding another's full effort, or enforcing requirements of social justice in the face of opposition. It may well be that a friend should point out another's self-pity parading as honesty, that a teacher should refuse to accept work that is beneath a given student's talents. A citizen may be called upon to point out a greed which masquerades as reasonable policy but which plunges many into hopeless poverty, or perhaps to suggest that behind an alleged patriotism lie prejudice, fear, and hatred of the stranger.

Perhaps the most powerful indication of this claim is found in reacting with horror to an atrocity to which we are vividly exposed. Our reaction from the pit of our stomach is simple and clear: This is wrong; this should not be done to a human being. It is quite remarkable, in fact, that attempts to justify inhuman treatment of people frequently appeal to the alleged subhuman status of the victim, as in racism, or to the other's alleged evil, as in war or in criminal prosecution. Beneath these arguments lies the experienced awareness that what is human and personal is to be respected and valued. Where one seeks to act otherwise, one must define the status of the victim as somehow less than human, less than good.

In experiencing the unconditional worth of a limited, fragile, perishable human being we experience the infinite source of that worth. In experiencing an inescapable claim upon us we experience the summons addressed from that source. That which summons us in and through the claim of another's worth is what is meant by God. The "will" of God need not be viewed as an arbitrary command imposed upon a situation from the outside. It is the call that comes to us from within and through another's worth, with its demands in a particular situation. Every human action in some way either denies or affirms human sacredness and thereby is a positive response to or a rejection of God. Our concept of and reply to God are most eloquently voiced in the way we treat other people.

Our belief in human dignity and in its divine source is most strongly tested and severely revealed in the ways we

deal with those who are least likely to have their dignity
recognized. These are the ones whom the Gospel calls the
least of the brothers. Among them in our society are the
elderly, the dying, the physically and mentally ill, the
handicapped, the economically deprived, the politically
powerless. Recognizing their worth does not mean senti-
mentally or condescendingly handing out goods, advice, or
cheerfulness to allegedly inferior beings. It means responding respectfully to the unmet needs of fellow human
beings, however much their intrinsic value is obscured for
us or difficult to find. One can respond in this manner only
if one has come to accept oneself as gift, as a person upon
whom everything, including one's very self, has been
bestowed.

As the Gospel makes clear, it is in responding to the least
of the brothers and sisters that one responds to that
ultimate mystery which Jesus addresses as Father. Incarnation means that it is in the flesh that one encounters God.
However great a treasure is held or concealed in such
earthen vessels, the vessels remain fragile. That is to say,
the flesh remains breakable and, in many cases, is actually
broken on the cross of life. To respond to those who are
broken is difficult. We are tempted to regard them as a
different breed and to set them aside from our mind and
sight. They mirror to us a dimension of ourselves which
threatens us. But the moral fiber of a society is perhaps best
indicated by the way it treats its weakest members.

Yet there are so many situations in which rights are
trampled, lives wasted or destroyed, and misery is so vast
that all talk of human sacredness seems utterly naive and
even cruel. Is this sacredness purely an illusion which only
those who are not so hungry or in so much pain can

sustain? To state that everything ultimately flows from and is drawn toward an infinite mystery which can be described in terms of love appears to be a horrible joke.

Nevertheless, the suffering and destruction of people can matter only if people matter. If human tragedy is no more significant than the blowing of dust in the wind, there is no basis of protest against it. Such protest makes sense only if there is a human worth in whose name it is lodged. The term "God" designates not an outsider who could but does not intervene in such situations but the presence already within the situation enabling and summoning us to hope and caring despite the strong pull toward despair and cynicism. Such attitudes will find expression in sharing the task of envisioning and creating an environment in which all people are more valued and are encouraged to value others, an environment in which trust is not undermined but made possible.

At the present time it is perhaps preferable to speak of the conscious and free response to human worth rather than to employ the somewhat vague and elusive concept of love of neighbor. This response is, in fact, the underlying requirement of all authentic human relationships, whether closely interpersonal or more widely social. But this fundamental attitude is most obviously reflected in the bonds of intimacy between two persons and especially in a marriage entered upon as a lifelong commitment.

In this instance, love branches into a cluster of qualities: an unconditional loyalty and faithfulness beyond caprice or passing fashion; an intimacy and tenderness free of flattery and self-assertion; a sense of sacrifice willing to bear the burdens of another and to forgive; a boundless openness to growth, superior to all the vicissitudes and perils of life;

a venturing trust in all that is as yet unknown and impenetrable in another; a oneness with the other that is not self-encasing but open toward others and one's society.

These and other qualities and the love which underlies them may at first be present only as a tenuous promise. They achieve a living reality only as they are hammered out on the anvil of everyday life, in its ordinariness and occasional grandeur, its joys and fears, its challenges and duties. For example, willingness to suffer for another becomes a reality in struggling to do so without bitterness and resentment. Forgiveness is attained when one's pain and anger do not strike out for revenge. Tenderness unfolds in quiet conversations when defensive walls are allowed to fall away. Fidelity takes shape as it resists being eroded by the wearisome little disappointments and failures of life. Only gradually and with much resistance does love as a basic attitude flow into all the sinews of one's being.

We have here the interplay between the core and layers, between the sculptor and the raw material of the person. Love flows from the core into a number of qualities, actions, and situations. It gradually leaves its imprint upon them and shapes them into its own expression, a symbol in which it is reflected. As we gather and confer our whole self from the heart upon another, we discover our true self, in its center and in its many dimensions. We find ourselves by giving ourselves away. We thereby also find the infinite, upon which our inmost core touches. To the extent that our self-giving proceeds from our very center and embraces all the dimensions of the self, it more clearly and tangibly mirrors the infinite. The presence within yet beyond our heart takes on flesh, so to speak. In Christian terms, the fullest expression, symbol, and incarnation of that presence is Jesus, the man filled with the Spirit, who is the way to the Father.

The integrating commitment of love is also directed to the other person in his or her totality and uniqueness. An authentic love does attend realistically to the specific demands of any given situation, as, for example, seeking medical assistance in time of serious illness. It does not, however, look to just one dimension of the other, such as appearance, personality, particular talent, or function. Individual responses are directed to the growth and fulfillment of the person as a whole, in his or her own way and for his or her own sake. At the same time, the gift of self reaches toward the heart of the other as a unique and irreplaceable person.

The core of the other is also a point of contact with the silent immensity which we call "God." The radical uniqueness of each person is not a blind alley but a door which opens onto a common infinite land. In reaching out to the heart of another, I discover the one mystery which envelopes us both. I learn that the source from which I reach and the goal to which I reach are one.

God is not an "added" being, "alongside" myself and another person. God is that which is within yet utterly distinct from the inmost kernel of the one who is loved, as well as from myself. In silence I discover myself as gift. In interpersonal love I discover the other as gift as well. I encounter the infinite oneness from and to which all flows and which, therefore, binds all together in solidarity. If I reach the depth of any person I discover a unique reflection, a word, of God.

We noted earlier that complete self-bestowal is a sharing of one's life, a sharing that reaches to the heart of the receptive other and remains there as a life-giving force. If God is to be conceived of as love, then God is present at the core of each person, enabling and calling forth to life. Once again, this presence within is totally other yet embodied in the man Jesus. God is the immanence of Spirit, the transcendence of Father, and the incarnation of Son.

Full personal commitment to another reaches into the future as well. Our deepest commitments are unconditional and irrevocable. Through them we define who we are and set the direction in which our life will unfold. In loving another in this way, we pledge ourselves to all that this love will imply or call for in the unknown future. We entrust ourselves beforehand to all that may emerge as unexpected or alien in the other, and despite all the hazards and changes in life. This is a venture in which we risk ourselves, for what will be demanded cannot be spelled out neatly in advance. It is a promise, therefore, which contains an unconditional and trusting surrender of oneself to the unknown.

This radical trust implies an underlying attitude to life and to reality as a whole. It implies that in being true to another we are most true to life: that life is such as to make this attitude possible and desirable. If so, then the ultimate context out of which we emerge as unique and relational persons is one which enables and evokes such trust. That context is trustworthy rather than indifferent or hostile. Our promise reaches in and through the other to that hidden trustworthiness which Jesus called Father. God is the mystery which comes to us from the unknown future, through the other person, and enables and summons our basic trust. Hence in the valuing, openness, fidelity, risk, and trust involved in the concrete love for another person, we experience and respond to the infinite future toward which we are drawn, beyond all that is finite.

Rahner (*Theological Investigations,* vol. 6, pp. 231-249) ties together these various strands by speaking of love as the basic act which sums up the whole essence of the person. If the person is one being, for all his or her many facets, there must be one such basic act. As distinctly human, it must involve awareness and freedom and must concern the realm of persons rather than things. Now, human knowing is always self-presence, the differentiation of self from environment. We see its highest form when the self emerges as a unique person set over against another person—the differentiation of an I from a Thou. The knowing process is completed by freely taking a stance toward this environment. This too is preeminently a free response to another person. In its positive form it is the conscious reunification of an I and a Thou, the love of another. In this continuing and developing process the awareness takes place in the light of the infinite, and the response is made in view of the infinite.

Thus the most basic human act is the conscious and free gift of one's unique self to another. In this act a person does finally experience, discover, and decide about who he or she is, about the other person, about the world as a whole, about life and its meaning, and about the all-enveloping infinite context. In this act one opens up in trusting love to the whole of reality and implicitly asserts that in love resides the ultimate wellspring and final goal of all reality. The reality from which we have emerged as unique beings and to which we entrust ourselves in loving another is ultimately to be described, not as nothingness, absurdity, indifference, or hostility, but as love. This view is not a naive romanticism or shallow optimism. It is a fundamental option which becomes a real conviction and hope only as it is tested and refined in the searing crucible of lived experience.

The experience of God through love complements the experience of God which comes through silence. In silence we experience our self as gift entrusted into our own hands. We shape that self most responsibly and fully by sharing it with another. Unless we possess ourselves in silence we cannot give ourselves. Unless we concretely give ourselves we will not discover ourselves. There is a basic rhythm of life here, as can be illustrated by a simple example. After we become totally engrossed in a play or film which really grips us, we do not normally wish to enter into a discussion the moment the curtain descends. We like to allow a time of quiet for the experience to sink in.

Our lives need moments of activity and involvement with others, moments in which we are totally present. They also need moments of solitary silence in which life can sink in and take root. Then the next spiral of involvement and silence can become richer and deeper. If we flee silence and merely keep busy while avoiding involvement, our lives will tend to be rootless and go around in circles. But if we follow this basic spiraling rhythm of involvement and withdrawal, speech and silence, action and contemplation, we will become more fully attuned and responsive to the infinite silence and infinite love within and beyond self and others.

It remains true, nevertheless, that even the fullest love for another, however much it is reciprocated, still fails to fill the deepest longing in our heart. The love for another fosters the conviction that life has meaning, but it does not provide the complete experience of that meaning. Our human longing is for an infinite meaning, glimpsed but not totally contained within human love. We come to a dead end if we try to make an absolute of human love or of the person loved. We do so as well if we try to bypass human love in our quest for an infinite meaning. The challenge is to grow toward an unconditional love of another without denying the other's finiteness. More generally, the challenge is to respond to the intrinsic worth of persons as unconditional yet as belonging to finite beings.

Similarly, this gift of self is bestowed upon one fragile and finite being by another. Despite our longing for and summons to love, there is ever the disappointment, fatigue, and pain of always falling short. We are also at times filled with agonizing doubts about our own worth. The moments when we do rise to a genuine concern for another are always felt as a kind of surprise, a gift. It is as though a power of love flowed through us rather than from us, somewhat as in giving birth a woman experiences the force of life surging through her.

In the heart of another we find a precious gift which calls for respect and caring. We also discover a deep yearning for worth, healing, and love, a yearning which may be riddled with self-doubt. The courage not to collapse in despair over human frailty is likewise a point of contact with the divine mystery. Where genuine love is in fact achieved, it is achieved in the hope that, despite all human questionableness and fragility, such a commitment to one's fellow human beings does make sense and need not meet with ultimate disappointment and futility. The term "God" then designates not only that which enables and summons us to such love, but also the presence which grounds and assures the hope of its final meaningfulness.

In summary, the infinite mystery from which we flow as precious gift and which summons us to respect the worth of others, especially the "least" ones, is what is meant by "God." In the experience of being valued with constancy and in discerning the claim of another to be equally valued, we are put in touch with a final truth about life. In learning to love another with the openness, trust, fidelity, generosity, and risk this entails, in struggling to grow beyond fear, anger, sorrow, failure, and in hoping for love's final significance despite our finite fragility, we meet and respond to God. That which enables and summons us to this response is the infinite love present in our hearts as Spirit, the infinite trustworthiness beyond them as Father, and the infinite truth made flesh in the Son who gave himself for others.

This love of another person, and indeed the very meaning and value of human life, appears threatened by the stark reality of death. At the same time, the response to human worth also has a more widely social dimension which looks to the conditions and structures within which people live, beyond the more obviously visible level of interpersonal bonds. Hence the next two chapters will deal respectively with the challenge of death and with the social dimension of love.

# CHAPTER EIGHT

# Death and Life

Our self is a gift, given into our own hands. We are free and are responsible for shaping it. We do so most creatively by bestowing it upon another. But self and other finally crumble in the dust of death. Is that the end of our story? Are we like a small curl of smoke or flicker of light, which makes its brief appearance and then is seen no more? Do we emerge as unique persons only to fall back into the anonymity of the elements which make us up and of the transient memories of those who remain for a short time after us? Is all our claim to sacredness, responsibility, and love nothing but a vain pretence? Is it a brief cry in the night before our voice is forever stilled?

Can there be meaning and hope in the face of death? Can we still trust in the unconditional meaningfulness of life despite its apparent collapse into nothingness? The stark realness of death seems at first sight to undermine everything that has been said so far. It poses the most severe challenge for the whole question of God. Nevertheless, the experience that one is still enabled and indeed summoned to hope despite death is an experience of God. God is the mystery we touch upon in the experience of being enabled and called to an active hope for life even out of death—not simply the one death at the end of life but the many deaths in the very midst of life.

In its most obvious sense, death refers to the bodily breakup which invariably and relentlessly comes to all persons. It is the cessation of all vital functions and of all distinctly human activity and relationships in the world, followed by biological dissolution. It is a brutal fact which remains outside the scope of our freedom. The truth that *I* have to die dawns early in life and, once present, can never be fully banished from my mind. It comes with the burgeoning awareness of myself as a distinct and therefore vulnerable, destructible person.

We may encounter death in a cruel and violent fashion as something inflicted, such as in the slaughters at concentration camps, the mass slayings in armed combat, or the ravages of starvation. These horrors may evince a terrified protest or an attempt to divert our attention. Any very sudden form of death readily provokes a certain sense of uneasiness and even shock in those who hear of it.

Yet dying quietly alone in the possibly impersonal atmosphere of a large public hospital can have its own terrors. We might well prefer to meet death in a familiar setting, surrounded by family and friends. Our very aversion to dying alone in a strange place amid unfamiliar faces brings out some of the harshness of death itself, and this aversion pushes us to desire the most supportive situation at the time. Because death is a collapse before which we are powerless, it can appear to us as a destructive fate which strikes us down from without.

Many features of death are brought home to us by the death of someone close to us. There is a strong sense of absence, as if the one who died has departed into silence from which no echo returns. Much of the pain of another's death springs from the impossibility of communication, accompanied by a realization of incompleteness. It is as if death had interrupted a conversation in the middle of a sentence. There remain many things left unsaid, many barriers still raised, many conflicts unresolved, more of oneself to share. This incompleteness can no longer be removed. At the same time, the radical uniqueness of the dead person becomes painfully clear, for no one can replace the one who has died.

These features come to the fore in the face of our own death. Beyond the physical anguish and pain we may suffer, an overwhelming loneliness can accompany our dying. No one else can live out our life for us. But even more unmistakably, no one else can die our death. There is also the loss of all we have held dear: the painful separation from those we have loved, the falling away of our life work, the departure from the physical world that has been our dwelling place. With these comes a sense of incompleteness, of loss, of forsakenness.

We need not negate the possibility of a peaceful and trusting death. But this is something to be achieved, not presumed. Trust is a letting go, which must always overcome some degree of uncertainty, fear, and difficulty. In dying we must let go of everything, and we can do so willingly only after a painful struggle.

Death is not merely an occurrence at the end of life; it pervades the whole of life. It becomes most manifest in illness, which can thwart all our plans for life and which brings home to us how little we can really foresee or control our own future. The helplessness which sickness imposes can diminish the capacity for thought, action, and relationship. It can cut off a person from society and its productive portion, so that he or she has a sense of being set apart, useless, and a burden to others. Illness is also difficult to integrate into the structure and thrust of one's life. It strikes us more as an interruption in living which can at best be endured. In ways such as these, suffering is a reminder, foreboding, and foretaste of death.

Death also makes itself felt in thousands of little ways. We meet it in the countless disappointments, failures, and losses woven into the fabric of our lives. We are forever having to say goodbye to persons and situations. The familiar is ever changing into the strange and alien. Beauty, goodness, and vitality are born in promise, only to pass away still unfulfilled. In many ways the path of life is an unfinished journey crisscrossed with sorrows. All these experiences are partial or miniature deaths. They point to the one death which ends our journey, however incomplete that journey may be.

Death and its foretaste in sickness and disappointment make jarringly apparent the radical incompleteness, contingency, and finiteness of human life. They also make more painfully clear the infinite longing which underlies our every experience. Death is the visible face of finiteness. It mirrors us to ourselves as finite beings in quest of the infinite. Yet it does so in a way which seems to negate our deepest longing.

It was noted earlier that we are questioning beings for whom our very self is a question. We must ask and decide about who we are and what we mean. We come into our own hands, however, as destined to die. The raw material we are given to shape consciously and freely is mortal and perishable. We must, therefore, decide about ourselves and our meaning within the awareness of our own dissolution.

As a biological fact, death is brutally unfree. As a human reality, death includes a person's understanding of and free response to this fate. Moreover, death calls everything into question. It sets forth in bold relief the very questionableness of life itself and confronts us with a radical choice. Is it possible to maintain the absolute value and meaning of human life, given its relentless course toward death? Or is death simply the final emptying out of life into absurdity and nothingness? The final alternatives are either unconditional hope in the meaning of life or total despair at its absurdity. Our lives may well fluctuate between these opposite poles, but they will, in the last analysis, move toward one or the other.

We need not repeat here the previous discussion of basic trust, unconditional worth, and total meaning. Some people do in fact live with these attitudes. They live out their existence with a conviction and love which do not capitulate as they face death. Their hope is experienced as a great gift for which they are deeply grateful. Unless we regard this gift of hope as an illusion, then that to which one is ultimately grateful and in which one ultimately hopes, however implicitly, is what is meant by "God." God is that which enables and summons us to absolute trust in the meaningfulness of life despite death. To accept our

mortal existence and to confide it to the silent infinity is to
experience, acknowledge, and respond to God.

The fundamental decision of hope or despair does not
take place only at the final moments of our physical life. We
may at that time be scarcely conscious or free at all. As with
the experience and awareness of death itself, our attitude of
hope or despair will pervade the whole of our lives. It will
be embodied, forged, and strengthened, not so much in
explicit ideas and words as in the actual living out of our
lives. Because of the very inevitability of death, mirrored
in all that is finite, our response can only be a yes or
a no, an acceptance or a rebellion, in the face of our own
powerlessness.

Refusal may take the form of a flight into diversion,
feverish activity, routine, anonymity, hollow religiosity,
superficial optimism, and the like. These are attempts,
unsuccessful in the end, to evade the issue. We may also
grasp at and frantically consume every possible experience
for fear of missing something and yet, at the last, taste
nothing but bitterness. We may try to accumulate all the
expensive trinkets of our society, cling to or dominate
other persons, and extend our political power into the
community. All these are attempts to build a protective
wall around our mortality, even though that wall is built
upon sand. These approaches all mask a despairing anxiety
over death, which may eventually give way to an angry,
mute, or cynical despair that is more explicit. They amount
to a confession that we cannot make sense of a life which
ends in death. Death then comes to one who cannot run
anymore, who cannot "take" anymore, and who thus, in
fright or bitterness, simply gives up. We are, of course,
painting an extreme picture here, but perhaps the seeds of

this reaction to death are found in all of us.

An attitude of trusting acceptance and hope will also take a variety of shapes. It will be especially carved out in the moments of disappointment, loss, failure, illness, or sorrow, both great and small, which are the many deaths in the midst of life. If we face rather than flee these difficulties, we may come to recognize that there is both promise and disappointment in everything we choose and attain. Nothing we gain ever exhausts our hope, which always reaches further. We may also realize, perhaps even in our greatest sadness, that no specific failure or loss necessarily spells a total disaster for us. Even when the thing or person we cherish most is taken away, it is possible to survive and grow and not to give up hope. Our hope may lie deeper than any loss.

Something but not everything is given in all we attain; something but not everything is taken away in all we lose. So it is possible to learn to experience deeply and then let pass, if necessary, rather than clutch desperately at the surface of life. We may give ourselves completely to the challenge, task, or person at hand. Yet we may do so with a willingness to let go, rather than with a need to cling or to force matters. In this response there is expressed, deepened, and perhaps discovered an underlying hope in the meaning of life despite death.

A strange and paradoxical awareness may be born out of struggling with the many deaths within life. We may gradually see that life is enhanced by sharing it, not by hoarding it. We grow by offering, not by refusing, ourselves. We do not find meaning and hope by clutching everything, grasping at others, and closing in on our walled-up self. Our life thrives and is enriched by opening and giving ourselves, by letting go of things and letting others be. A wider and deeper aliveness is found by facing, enduring, and going beyond the pains and sorrows of life.

In this light we may understand hope (in the sense of an underlying attitude) as an orientation to life. It is a hope for life, for a fullness of life, a life fully alive and meaningful. More than that, it is a hope for a fullness of life even out of death. To truly hope is to be convinced that somehow out of death, in its many senses and forms, new life can be born.

We consider someone's hope to be strong if it has been tried and tested by all the negativities which life can hurl at a person. These are a crucible in which hope is either purified or consumed. If one's hope is destroyed, lost, or given up, one dies interiorly. It is as if a light within had gone out, leaving total darkness, or as if the substance were gone and only the shell remained. Despair is death within life. Hope is life even out of death. In this profound sense, hope is resurrection.

A person who has been hurt, deprived, or frightened too early and too often may lack sufficient security and self-esteem to allow him or her to discern light in the darkness or to view giving as other than total loss. To the extent that a consumer society fosters greed and opposition among people, it reinforces this view and behavior. The contrary vision, which stresses life emerging out of death and flowing into generosity, is possible, but it is difficult and will always involve struggle. Thus hope is not only the conviction that out of death new life *can* be born; it also includes the struggle to bring that new life to birth.

Out of the experience of grappling with the pain of life, therefore, may emerge a fundamental trust which gives us a vision of life as meaningful and which encourages in us a generous openness and gift of self. In other words, a faith and love emerge which are grounded in hope. In traditional theology, these are the three divinely bestowed theological virtues which unite us directly to the gracious God. That is, in this underlying conviction, basic trust, and gift of self we encounter and respond to God. God may be portrayed as the ultimate reality which enables and summons us to hope for life in its fullness, even out of death, and to translate that hope into our vision and behavior.

There is no question here of a kind of outside divine ruler who either delights in inflicting pain upon humans or else magically shields them from all sorrow and struggle. Nor is it a question of our either reveling in suffering or, conversely, making our lives a flight from being hurt. What is at issue is how we respond to the inevitable painfulness in human life. If we sense that life, with all its pain, can and should be lived with hope, we discern within that experience a gift and call. The term "God" need not refer to an outside intervener. It points rather to a presence touched upon within the experience itself: the source and goal, at once within and beyond that gift and call.

We find here a clue to understanding the familiar notion of God as all-powerful. All too often, power is imaged as physical violence, personal domination, or political tyranny. In that view, it is the capacity to dominate, destroy, or put to death. But a different image of power can be found in agriculture, parenthood, teaching, therapy, music conducting, and the like. Here it means the capacity to create, to foster growth, to set free, the capacity to bring something to life, either originally or more fully. And the fullest power lies in the ability to bring something to life even out of death, to create where destruction has reigned.

Seen in this light, the "all-powerful" God is that presence at the heart of existence which enables and summons
us to the fullness of life, even out of the many deaths in the
midst of life, and perhaps out of the one death at the end of
life. As generative source of such life even out of death,
God is called Father. As embodied in a man of hope whose
vision and love persist even unto death on a cross, God is
called Word or Son. As presence within us urging to such
hope, God is called Spirit.

Such hope will be most at stake in those situations where
our vision seems unsure, our love unprofitable, or our
immediate hopes dashed. Jeremiah, for example, remained
true to his vision and vocation even though it made him a
man of sorrows. Hosea continued to love despite rejection,
desertion, and infidelity. Job suffered the loss of everything
but his hope.

As these examples suggest, this hope reaches out of
ourselves to others as well. All our contacts with others, in
some small way at least, either respond to or negate their
value. We either call something to life in others or put
something to death. Love was previously depicted here as
the gift of one's own aliveness which brings something to
life in another. Hatred, by contrast, refuses one's life to
another and even in some fashion takes the other's life. The
fullest love is that which brings something to life in
another who has interiorly died or been killed, the "least"
one. Such love also looks to the institutions and structures
of society, seeking to reform or change those which inflict
death in its many forms and to promote those which are
life-furthering. God is that infinite "power" which enables
and summons us to a love which brings forth life, even out
of death.

We may add a brief word on the question of evil, although no answer ever really satisfies mind or heart. The question is often asked in terms of how a good and all-powerful God could allow the wanton destruction and evil which afflict human history. The image of God is that of an outside agent who could but does not intervene and come to the rescue; God is presumed to be absent from the situation.

In the light of the foregoing approach we may pose the question in a different way. Is it possible in the face of evil to overcome the despair which surges in us and not to give up hope? Is it possible to sustain hope for others and to assist them in their struggle with tragedy and despair? Is this even a task to which our conscience calls us? What possibility and demand do we find in our deepest self in the presence of evil and suffering? Do we find ourselves enabled and summoned to bring hope out of despair, life out of death?

If we do so, we are expressing the conviction that there is a reality deeper than death and despair, a reality which impels us toward life and hope. That deeper reality, within yet beyond us, from which flow this gift and call to hope, is what is meant by "God." Rather than applying from without a preconceived notion of God, we discover God present within the situation and its challenge, and we fashion our concepts in its light, guided by our religious tradition.

We turn again to the final death at the end of life. Can this also be a death out of which life emerges? Can the complete surrender of self which is demanded here be a finding of self as well?

Certainly those who give their lives for others in some form of martyrdom do express this hope. They believe that their dying has a worthwhile and lasting effect, that their death is a source of life for others. Now, their dying is very obviously an act in which their whole self is involved and at stake. They are thus implicitly affirming a lasting meaning for that self. This is the basic drive of hope in the face of physical death: that one's life have a meaning which endures. It is the hope that out of one's life as a whole which ends in death, something of lasting worth may be born or brought to life. In this sense, it is a hope for "resurrection" and "eternal" life. It is a longing that the self which we fashion out of the raw material of our life be a lasting work of art. This question of enduring validity is distinct from that of the survival of individual consciousness and freedom. It provides the proper relational and communal context in which the latter question can be viewed.

The desire for an enduring meaning shines forth clearly in the wish to be remembered and in the fear of being forgotten. Children, for example, make forthright bids for attention and are much hurt when chosen last or not at all for a game. Many elderly persons are plagued by the fear that no one will remember them after they are "gone," especially if they have no children or none who cares, no home or community to which they feel a sense of belonging. People engage in many activities precisely to be noticed and remembered. At a time of separation, one of the deepest expressions of love is the promise never to forget the other. In its most authentic expression the longing to be remembered is the desire to make our life something worth remembering, the desire that our life be of lasting benefit, at least for others.

This desire is also reflected in the situation of one who

finds out that he or she has a very short time to live. The initial reaction may be one of utter shock and disbelief, possibly one of fear and even terror as the reality sinks in, followed by anger and resentment because one does not want to die yet. Afterward, in coming to grips with the situation, the person may look to the brief interlude remaining. Unless prevented by weakness, one may wish to make a last trip to a favorite spot or to visit for the first and last time some special place that one has longed to see. This wish suggests the desire to complete our life's journey before life is over. We want, before death, to gather together and complete our lives.

We may also seek at this time to tell our life story to another who will listen and appreciate, or to convey our final wisdom and desires to our children. We wish to have our story told again after its author is gone; we wish to continue to be remembered and to exert an influence. There is also a hint or awareness here that whatever of ourselves remains unshared somehow perishes; that only what is bestowed upon others somehow endures. This again reflects the paradox that only life which is given away is truly alive. Love alone has the power to bring something or someone to life in an enduring way. There is within us a longing to give our whole gathered self in a way that is truly memorable.

When death is imminent we may similarly wish to see a minister or priest and to be reconciled to family and friends. We may realize that much untruth and wrongness is still present in our life. With this painful sense of the brokenness within ourselves and of our alienation from others comes a desire for "at-one-ment." We long for a newness of life out of that especially devastating form of death which is sin. We are drawn to overcome whatever fragments and divides us. We want to be forgiven, healed, and made whole within ourselves. We want to be at one with others and with our surrounding world.

Within this experience of the approach of death we touch upon what is meant by "God." God is that which draws us to the total gathering and gift of self beyond all brokenness and betrayal. God is the dynamic oneness which is the ground and goal of all wholeness, oneness, and atonement. God is that into whose hands we are called to commend our dying self, with the hope that out of this final death may issue forth something of lasting value: eternal life.

We might at first be inclined to think that our desire for enduring meaning would be met if we had unending life on earth without physical death. If we look more closely, though, we see that our longing does not really lie in this direction. Aside from all the other difficulties implied in such a situation, it would mean that every decision could be postponed and replaced countless times. None would be crucial. All would be indifferent, empty, without significance. This scenario is reflected in many science fiction stories of an imagined future without physical death.

Our freedom as we experience it now, however, is the crucial capacity and challenge to put our self totally and irrevocably into a decision, to fashion ourselves once and for all. The threat of life's brevity is that our lives remain incomplete, unshared, broken. The longing which death's imminence brings home to us is to complete, share, and reconcile our self. What is critical is to finish this task, not merely to prolong it. Our desire for enduring meaning is a longing that the "finished" self have a final and lasting validity, worth, and meaning.

Once we move the question of hope from the realm of an enduring validity, in general and for others, to that of life out of death for our own unique personal center, matters become more difficult. In the light of what we have discovered, we cannot portray any such hope as a desire to return to the womb or to the present earthly situation. Rather than regression or endless recurrence, the quest would be for a consummation, a birth into a new life which escapes visualization. To cite an example from nature, the caterpillar does not enter the cocoon in order to re-emerge as a caterpillar, let alone an egg, but to come forth as a butterfly.

We sometimes raise this question of "new" life by means of the concepts of time and eternity, pictured in terms of duration. Time is viewed as a fairly brief span, at least when seen as a lifespan. Eternity is pictured as a literally interminable period of time. Both are readily seen as the ticking away of moments on a clock, something external to us, against which we may be measured.

We might more profitably look at time and eternity as dimensions of our present human experience. From this angle, time is the experience of our own becoming. It is felt as the process of tending, moving, and striving toward a goal. It is found in the sustained effort to progressively learn a skill in one specific area of life, such as athletics, music, or career training. More generally, time is experienced in the process of gradually gathering our whole self into our hands in order to achieve the goal of our life as a whole.

Eternity, by contrast, may be linked to the experience of being rather than becoming, of "being all there" rather than "getting there." It is the sense of being totally present rather than reaching for what is still ahead of us. It is felt in those rare moments of life when we are totally caught up in something: a moment of new insight which transforms our understanding, of unspeakable closeness to another, of total absorption in music performed or heard, of silent oneness with the universe. In these instants we are oblivious to the passage of time. We do not think about ourselves, yet we are totally self-present because we are totally involved. We are more whole and united than we have ever been. These are transfiguring moments when all is turned to light before sinking back once more into everyday obscurity. These are the truly memorable occasions when the power of the universe pulsates through us in truth, love, beauty, and peace.

The biblical image of a throng of people joined with choirs of angels singing before the heavenly court may point to this dimension of experience. We need not think here of an unending church service. We can call to mind instead the experience of being completely taken over by a piece of music. We are caught in the flow of something wide and beautiful whose sound echoes the heart of the universe itself. The biblical image (see Revelation, chapters 4 and 5) may point to the totally involving and transforming experience, shared by and with others, of being tuned in completely to the infinite mystery.

Within this context we may now rephrase the question of a new life out of the final death for the personal self we have fashioned and bestowed. In the special moments of life when we are totally present and transfigured, do we touch upon an ultimate truth? When the process of becoming, which is our present life, comes to an end, do we begin a new life of totally being what we have become? If such a hope is possible, then that which sustains, receives, and fulfills this hope is what is meant by "God." We may point to the infinite mystery with terms such as total or infinite being, life, presence: the God who is, who was, and who will be.

This hope for enduring meaning for self and others is possibly the basic experience which underlies the many scriptural statements about remembering. We are told that the just will be remembered and the wicked forgotten. Yahweh is said to remember his people, along with the gifts and promises made to them in the past. The recollection of God's dynamic and gracious presence in the past is linked to a hope for similar mindfulness in the present and future. He is called upon not to forget his people in their present need and to remember them on the last day and forever.

If we are remembered we do not totally vanish. The world has become forever different because we have existed. If we are "remembered" by the infinite mystery, we are remembered unconditionally, in our unique and total self which is uttered from and summoned by this mystery. We do not pass away but somehow remain.

If we may experience ourselves as gift rather than as fluke, we do have meaning. If we are a gift to last, a gift to be remembered, then we have an enduring meaning. If we are given by name and called by name, we may also be remembered by name, that is, in our very uniqueness and personal meaning. To be remembered is also a gift which is freely given. We cannot take such a possible gift, but only be open to receive it. Our openness shows in our trust

before death. That to which we confide our entire self and
life, in basic trust and in the face of death, is what is meant
by "God." If we die with trust, we die into God. Perhaps
that is as much as we can and should say.

Our underlying sense of hope reaches toward a fullness
of life for ourselves and others, a life which is fully alive,
meaningful, and glimpsed in certain rare moments. Our
longing takes us beyond anything finite, which can neither
sustain nor shatter this hope, into the infinite. We tend
toward a life which is born even out of death and which has
meaning that endures. Yet we are powerless before a
physical death we can neither prevent nor fully understand.
When we have gone to the limit of our powers we can only
turn our outreach into an openness to receive. Our hope is
for the gift of infinite, eternal life; it reaches toward a
source and goal of life beyond all that is finite and mortal,
beyond all death. This source and goal is God.

We encounter God within this experience of hope and
can speak of God in its light. If we are able to hope in this
unconditional way, then that upon which this hope rests
and that toward which it tends is what is meant by "God."
If we scan human history and come upon Jesus, we may see
that this man embodies the hope which arises in the core of
our being, and that he does so in the face of a cruel and early
death for others, offered to the Father. If our hope is not in
vain, it is found in Jesus. Thus the Christian tradition says
that he has passed to life out of death, that he is risen.

In the next chapter we will turn more directly to the
social aspects of the deepest human experience.

# CHAPTER NINE

# The Human Future on Earth

Each person is a unique gift who is given, called, and remembered by name. Each has an unconditional worth and a lasting meaning. We are each responsible for shaping this precious gift. We do so most creatively by bestowing it upon others, with a trusting hope in the future despite the reality of death. In all these spheres, we encounter and respond to the infinite mystery we call "God."

We have been paying more attention to what is distinctly personal (in the sense of individual) in awareness, freedom, love, and hope. Yet the experience of these is inseparably social as well. In this chapter we will focus directly upon the social dimension of our deepest experience and the God to whom it points. Out of these considerations comes an approach to God as the presence which enables and summons us to build a more truly human future on earth and to do so with and for others, with hope in its lasting significance.

As previously noted, we emerge as unique selves within

a physical and social context which both nurtures and mars us. We make our decisions and commitments within this setting, especially before the persons and groups whose lives impinge upon our own. In loving we respond to the intrinsic worth of another human being. That worth addresses its claim to us in everyone we meet, not only in intimate situations but also in those which are more widely social. Hope includes the desire that the self we fashion and bestow have a life-giving and enduring value for others and for our whole world.

This social context from which we emerge and to which we respond will, at its various levels, be predominantly supportive or predominantly undermining of positive vision, relationships, and hope. Our own free attitude and action will also leave their own chiefly destructive or creative impact upon this environment. So we need to assess the institutions and conditions which prevail in our society to discern their effect upon ourselves and others and the possible influence we can and do have upon these social factors. Insofar as they fall within our awareness and freedom they also lie within the scope of our responsibility.

If the whole preceding perspective is valid, then we are indeed called, according to our capacity and opportunity, to strive to achieve a society in which people are enabled and encouraged to live with a greater conviction of life's meaningfulness, a fuller self-esteem and generous concern for others, and a stronger trust in life's final and lasting value. Conversely, we are challenged to overcome situations in which pain or narrowness shrinks horizons, rivalry and hatred destroy friendship, and hope is shattered. We are summoned to do so with a special concern for the weaker members of society. In terms of our approach, that upon which this call rests and to which it replies is what is meant by "God." God is that infinite presence which enables and summons us to the task of building a more truly human society on earth.

Without entering into great detail we will elaborate on some social dimensions of conscious responsibility, love, and hope, following the order of the preceding presentation. In the process we will at once presuppose and broaden a little the concepts of God already developed.

Our basic decisions about ourselves take place in the inmost center of our being. Then, like ripples from a stone dropped in a pond, they gradually extend to all the layers of our makeup and into our outward activity, where they make their impact upon other persons and upon our overall surroundings. Our deepest inner acts reach out in time also. Through them we gather up our past and decide who we irrevocably are and will be. They reach into our own future and also influence the future of others and of the world in which we live. In this vein, folktales often delight in recounting a long chain of actions and reactions triggered by a seemingly innocuous gesture.

In previous eras the ripples of inner decisions did not seem to extend very far. They quickly washed up against the walls of an apparently unchangeable natural and social order. Social position was largely defined ahead of time. The world of nature was like an unalterable stage upon which people played out their lives. Outward changes occurred so slowly as to be virtually imperceptible, so that people experienced themselves as essentially continuing the past. (This portrait is, of course, greatly oversimplified for the sake of brevity.)

The modern breakthrough of science and technology

has dramatically altered this situation. The human race no longer so much *lives within* its outer environment as *changes* it. The extent of rapid external change is obvious in a glance at photographs spanning the past century. This change is the result of human intervention. The world of nature now seems more like a quarry which provides the materials and site for humanity to construct a world of its own choosing. Developments in the life sciences and social sciences place many regions of our genetic and psychic makeup within human hands. We are also aware that our social institutions do not reflect a preordained order but are the changeable products of human decision. Moreover, as change accelerates it becomes visible, as in time-lapse photographs of a flower's growth. We no longer experience ourselves as continuing a familiar past but as moving into an open and therefore uncertain future. This situation is reflected in the rise of science fiction as a literary form.

As a consequence, within its finite limits human freedom in general moves more and more beyond the sphere of purely interior attitudes into their practical application in the material, social, and historical realms. The ripples, so to speak, emanate farther before they are dissipated and contained. The creation of our own environment becomes more a matter of human responsibility.

If human decisions are not confined to inner attitudes but bring about changes in the world around us, they become more visible. The decisions and their effects are right before us: an orchard in a once-barren desert, a dying lake that once teemed with fish. As a result, the experience of responsibility, in all its inescapable, crucial, and unconditional character (discussed above), can become even more acute. To that extent we may also sense more vividly, if implicitly, the ground and goal of such responsibility, the listening silence before which we are ultimately accountable.

In earlier ages the experience of a constant natural and even social order provided a fund of images and concepts of God. Today it is not so much nature as the responsibility for shaping it which may do so. The image of God was once quite spontaneously linked to a world which people could not greatly fathom or affect. Nature was readily experienced (in a way that is less accessible to us today) as majestic and powerful, at once fascinating and awesome: a sacred realm indwelt by a divine presence.

At present, nature no longer appears to be the house of God but a vast and empty space, for the most part, which we try to fill with airplanes, rockets, and space probes. What is within this space is seen primarily as material which is at our human disposal. It falls within, rather than stands over against, our freedom. In this world we discover little, if anything, which speaks to us of God. Our imprint is already upon it to the extent that we discern only our own image. Human responsibility rather than nature is thus our more immediately available springboard for the concept of God.

Moreover, appropriately exercising responsibility in a changeable situation is different from exercising it in an unchangeable one. We respond differently, for instance, to a poison for which there is an antidote than we do to an incurable illness. If life is meaningful, then situations we cannot change, whether of suffering, death, or even a certain social condition, call for acceptance. In those that we can change, whether quickly or gradually, the meaning lies in changing them positively. As ultimate ground and

goal of meaning, God is that infinite presence which
summons us not only to accept things but also to creatively
change them.

The Gospel shows Jesus healing the sick, not just
helping them to die. It also shows him wrestling with and
accepting his own death. The call of God challenges us to
distinguish what is to be accepted from what is to be
modified, and to act accordingly with courage. Today, both
natural and social factors fall much more considerably
within the ambit of the changeable.

To the extent that we can change natural and social
factors, we can picture these as given to us or coming into
our own hands. In former ages when the universe seemed
much smaller, it was easier to picture God as one being
within that world, almost as one of its inhabitants, and yet
its architect and ruler as well. Today, however, we know
the universe to be so unimaginably vast that even if we try
to picture God as part of our world, God still seems to be an
immensely distant alien. Hence it is better to think of God,
not as one being among others in the world, but as the
unseen ground of the world as a whole, utterly before and
beyond the world. Yet in this imagery God is also very near
as that from which our very self and the entire world flow,
and flow as gift rather than fluke. God is likewise that
toward which this world tends, in and through us humans.
In the words of Paul, all of creation groans in the labor of
childbirth, expecting to see itself and us born into the
freedom of God's children (Romans 8:19-23).

Today this gift is given into human hands in an un-
dreamed-of way. It is a sacred trust, etched by the centuries,
which is to be moulded for the good of persons and finally
confided into the infinite mystery. In the light of an

evolutionary viewpoint, we might say that all reality is drawn to reach beyond itself, and in and through humanity to reach for the infinite. That from which this dynamic, striving process ultimately flows and that toward which it ultimately reaches is what is meant by "God."

Despite this further-reaching freedom and responsibility, many people do in fact feel more powerless than ever before to affect their own physical and social environment. They regard themselves as victims of such forces as the massiveness of modern industry and government, the machinations of international politics and commerce, and the interaction of all kinds of complex social factors which no one seems able to understand or control. Here too we must acknowledge the responsibility for our own inner attitude toward any such situation. At the same time it is important not to look for a pretext to evade responsibility or to justify a lack of concern. Nor should we, on the other hand, take on more burdens than we can bear, or batter ourselves against unyielding barriers. What is crucial is to determine honestly the concrete possibilities and limits of our responsibility, without either self-pity or messianic illusions.

Hence the term "God" points to the ultimate ground and term of human responsibility, now seen as the dynamic presence which enables and summons us to discern and share in the task of shaping our natural and social environment, insofar as it is given into our hands.

Just as the free shaping of our self is fulfilled by bestowing it upon others, so too the shaping of our world must be directed to persons as intrinsically valuable. Because of the more intimate connotations of the term "love," we might more accurately speak of "the free response to human worth" when we deal with the broader communal, social contexts in which people live out their lives. The challenge is to channel our response toward the good of the unique person, the whole person, and all persons. That which ultimately enables and summons us to this social gift of self is what is meant by "God."

The love for any individual looks to all the dimensions and contexts of that person's existence; it does not just regard him or her in isolation. To cite an extreme case, we do not quietly converse with one whose house is burning. More plausibly, parental care for a child is more than a matter of direct exchanges between them. It also involves the creation of a home, a climate within which the child can unfold. This concern will similarly extend to the conditions in the neighborhood, the school, and *all* the contexts which play a part in the child's formation.

Our concern for any person must, therefore, consider the physical, familial, economic, political, cultural, religious, and other settings which greatly affect his or her life. In considering all these we need to ask whether and to what degree each context is life-furthering or death-dealing, whether it responds to human sacredness or treats people chiefly as functions, merchandise, or disposable things. To what extent does that social structure, institution, or condition tend to bring something to life physically, emotionally, intellectually, morally, religiously, or in any other way in the person, and to what extent does it tend to diminish or destroy life in any of these ways?

Our task, according to our capacity and opportunity, is to more and more transform these contexts into life-furthering environments. In this regard a truly therapeutic community is one in which life is nurtured in those who have been put to death in some of the above ways. Infant baptism can be viewed in this light rather than as a ritual which magically transforms the child. It may be seen as a pledge on the part of the parents and the community to do all they can to gradually bring this child to a fullness of life. They do so because of, and in response to, the power of life out of death embodied in the man Jesus. The Church may also be looked upon from this angle as the community in which people call one another to life by sharing such things as bread and forgiveness.

It is certainly in being cared about as an individual and in caring about another that we most fully discover and respond to the unique and human sacredness of ourselves and the other. But that sacredness belongs to *every* person simply because he or she is a human being, though we usually discover it only in the persons we come to know intimately. The genuine caring for any human being impels us toward respect for all human beings, whatever limits may be imposed upon the practical expression of that respect. This thrust will also push us toward concern with the life-giving and life-taking qualities of ever-wider social contexts. It has often been said that the Gospel cannot be preached to the hungry. It might also be said that the Gospel is preached in part by feeding the hungry. More than that, it might be said that the Gospel is also preached by working to change conditions which lead to people's being hungry.

The fulfillment of our own uniqueness does not consist in narrowly closing in upon ourselves or in trying to gratify our own personality with the aid of one or a few others, even though anxiety and defensiveness may push us in this direction. However, marriages and small communities which attempt to become ends in themselves invariably flounder. They flourish only if they have a focus or goal beyond themselves. The openness of those who in a special way belong together must reach out to others with an openness which, in principle, extends to all persons, since all are to be valued.

In experiencing both the unconditional worth of oneself, of the friend, of the stranger, and in experiencing also the claim that worth places upon us, we touch upon its ultimate ground and term, which we call "God." Thus we are called not only to be a life-giving presence to others individually but also to strive to transform our many social contexts: to discard or reform those that are life-destroying and to develop and strengthen those that are life-fostering. More than that, we are summoned to reach ever past the limits of our present caring and concern.

The scriptural challenge to love the stranger and the enemy means, in effect, that we cease regarding others as aliens and as objects of hostility. Such a view is neither a sentimentality which glosses over real conflicts nor a self-styled martyrdom which naively exposes itself to another's hostility. It is rather an invitation to struggle with our prejudices, our divisions, and our hostilities.

But how we do move toward an environment more in keeping with the intrinsic worth of each person, the whole person, and all persons? Any attempt to modify social structures not only runs into disagreement as to how and whether it should be done but meets with active resistance as well. Just as we encounter conflict within ourselves, so we find it among individuals and groups. What does response to human worth mean in a situation of conflict? How does one oppose another without denying his or her claim to respect?

Persons who attempt to build a society more expressive of human worth certainly cannot begin by presuming to use means which contradict the end. They must first address themselves to the understanding and freedom of those they seek to influence. Priority will be given to communication and cooperation rather than to deceit and domination. We know of situations on an individual level, however, in which insight and freedom are either lacking or are turned toward destructive activities. Hence we seize the child before he or she runs into the path of an oncoming car, and we disarm the emotionally distraught person. In institutional matters involving much larger groups, the situation is far more complex. At the very least we should strive to reduce the areas of disagreement in which physical force or violence is used; otherwise the society we build is hardly more truly human. At the same time any renewed or new structures must attempt to include opponents, not obliterate them. We do not overcome an injustice inflicted upon us by inflicting that injustice upon another. We overcome it only by creating a situation in which this kind of act is less likely to occur. The aim is to establish a human society in which differences are respected and integrated, and conflicts are resolved mutually and without violence.

The social dimension of "love of neighbor," then, involves struggle and strives for a unity which includes and yet goes beyond plurality and conflict. From this standpoint, God is not to be portrayed as a magical supplier of answers from without but as the mysterious presence within yet beyond the situation—a presence which enables and summons us to deal with the questions themselves, to engage in, to struggle with, and even perhaps to agonize over these matters. Nor is God to be depicted as the God "on our side" brought in to justify our animosities and to support our activities against the other side. God is rather the ultimate oneness which is fullness, from which all flows and to which all is drawn; a oneness which gathers, preserves, integrates, reconciles, and goes beyond all differences, polarities, and divisions; a oneness which summons our response beyond all conflict and hatred.

Our shaping and our gift of self are made with the hope of their enduring meaning. The same is true of our shaping the world for the sake of human persons. We turn now to the larger social dimension of our experience of hope.

Hope is a reaching out of the present into the future for a fuller life for self and others. It includes an openness to growth beyond where we are now, and indeed, beyond all that is finite. In intimate personal bonds and smaller communities it implies both a reaching beyond the present situation of the relationship and a shared reaching into goals beyond the community itself. In the wider social sphere it implies a willingness to grow beyond the present conditions and institutions.

In individual relationships we can never regard the other person as the total fulfillment of our life. The same applies to our social setting. To look upon any particular institution, structure, or social condition as the answer to all our needs, the solution to all our problems, the gratification of all our desires, is idolatry. None can therefore be regarded as utterly immutable, beyond question or criticism. All can and must be continually called into question and subjected to creative scrutiny and evaluation.

At the same time, intimate personal love does foster the conviction that life is meaningful, even though such love does not provide a complete experience of life's meaning.

Similarly, while not ultimate themselves, the various social contexts either promote or militate against the conviction of life's meaning; they either nurture hope or push toward despair.

We experience these present contexts as finite because we see them in the light of the infinite toward which our hope is ultimately drawn. More immediately, we assess them in the light of a creative vision, however imprecise or obscure, of the future human society. Through working to implement that vision we also express the hope that reaches beyond the present. It is indeed by our very efforts to bring about this envisioned society that our hope becomes concretely real.

In the experience, then, of being called to reach beyond, to question, and to shape our environment in a direction which fosters meaning and hope for those who dwell in it, we touch upon the God of hope.

Our striving to build a better human future also implies a human rather than a mechanical sense of time. The future in question is not simply one which happens of itself at a later date. It is one which is wrought through struggle and effort, often involving painful conflict and serious doubt as to the proper course of action. It is not an inevitable process but a future conceived and brought to birth out of human decision and action. Once again, this human future must not sacrifice the present generation to the next but must be built upon respect for the dignity of those now living, especially the "least" ones.

Nevertheless, every society which we help to build will always be fashioned from finite materials and composed of finite persons. Hence, it will not only be promise but disappointment, because nothing finite, no matter how

new or improved, can fill the scope of human longing.
Moreover, just as we and those we love most will die, so too
the human future we share in bringing to birth will also
pass away. We encounter again, this time in a wider
context, the question of enduring meaning. This too we
cannot guarantee. We can only reach out in openness to
receive as gift the lasting significance of our world and
our self.

If we can strive for the humanizing transformation of
our environment with a conviction of its lasting value, and
if we can reach in trust, however implicitly, toward that
source of meaning, then in so doing we encounter and
respond to what is meant by "God." That from which we
receive self and world, that which enables and summons us
to transform it, and that to which we are called to entrust it
in hope for its lasting significance—this is what is meant
by "God."

We might also extend our glance to include the entire
human community, past, present, and future, and its total
physical environment, and ask about its meaning and
purpose. We might form a similar portrait of one human
being who stands for all. Into his or her hands has come a
self, a society, a world, all as gift. This person accepts the
gift, gathers it up, transforms it by his or her vision, love,
and hope, and raises it as an offering. That from which all
flows as gift, and that to which it is called to return as
transformed offering, is what is meant by "God," the alpha
and omega, the originating ground and absolute future of
all that is. If we envision that one human being as Jesus,
then perhaps we sense what Paul means by the recapitula-
tion of all things in him (Ephesians 1:10).

To sum up, in striving to build as life-giving a social

order as possible, we fulfill our inescapable responsibility, make a loving response to persons as being of intrinsic worth, and express a trusting hope for the lasting meaning of self, humanity, and even all creation. In so doing, we touch upon God as enabling and summoning us to this response.

The shaping of self and world according to vision and conviction, the direction of this task to the good of human persons, and the hope for its lasting meaning, are offset and countered by a pull in the opposite direction. This is the reality of sin to which we have already made scattered references. As a result of sin, the path we have traced is always a painful overcoming, a reaching from betrayal to response. It always involves a forgiveness and healing which enable and summon us from blindness, hatred, and despair to enlightenment, reconciliation, and renewed hope. Hence as our final topic we will consider the God of forgiveness and healing.

# CHAPTER TEN

# Forgiveness and Healing

We are each a sacred and responsible person, summoned to share ourself with others and to build a more human society, with hope for lasting meaning despite the death of all individuals and cultures. Yet pervading these dimensions of life is an experience that seems to undermine them: that of sin.

We find ourselves drawn to spurn the precious gift that we are, to make decisions contrary to our own inmost self, to wound and betray others, to ignore and contribute to the strife and injustice in society, and so to cut away any enduring meaning. We experience, in other words, the sinfulness which infects ourselves and our world. This violation afflicts us deeply. It moves us to reach out for a forgiveness of our heart and a healing of our whole self and of our world. That which we touch upon as ultimately betrayed by our sin and as ultimately sought after for forgiveness is what is meant by "God."

To explore the awareness of God disclosed through this

tragic experience, we will first inquire into sin and its implications. We will then look into the acknowledgement of sin and its forgiveness, the suffering that sin entails, and the healing it requires. We will follow roughly the same sequence as before, considering sin in relation to conscious freedom, love, and hope, in their intimate personal and broader social dimensions.

In everyday speech, a person is commonly regarded as "guilty" if he or she breaks a rule or law of some kind. It may be a family custom or a civil code; it may be written or spoken, grave or trifling. A person may be guilty, for example, of a breach of etiquette, a traffic violation, a theft of property, or an assault on another individual. In all these cases, the common element is anoutward action contrary to a rule or law.

In a slightly more general sense, guilt is associated with an action that meets with disapproval. The more serious the matter, the less the disapproval seems arbitrary or linked to specific circumstances. The action is seen as not to be done at all, or done only under extreme circumstances. The infliction of death, disfigurement, or other grave injury or loss is most often looked upon in this way. In such cases the actions of others are judged to be wrongful, independently of the doer's whims, intentions, or even good faith. In its strongest sense, guilt is associated with actions which are wrong in themselves.

Where serious blame is attached and a penalty is imposed in a legal setting, it is assumed that the culprit is free and responsible for his or her action. If the one committing a criminal offence is a child or a person afflicted by severe mental illness, the matter is treated differently, since both unlawful behavior and free responsibility are essential to legal guilt.

With freedom we enter the interior realm of the person. Yet not everything within is free. We spoke before of the many factors which affect our attitudes as well as our actions. These include the more intimate influence of family and friends as well as that of our wider social contexts. These factors may be positive or negative. In terms of the earlier discussion, they are negative insofar as they "kill" something in the person or, in general, foster a sense of worthlessness and of not belonging.

These factors reduce the level of freedom. They produce inner conflict, pain, illness, desperation, and hostility, which push a person toward conduct destructive to self and others. Here "guilt" can designate these inner feelings of self-rejection that pronounce a verdict of worthlessness and impose a sentence which takes life away. This kind of guilt is independent of how a person behaves, and it can be intensified by trivial actions. By contrast, positive influences enhance the level of freedom and develop a more objective sense of responsibility.

In this light we move toward an idea of sin as a wrong or destructive action which is freely done. Many might object here and say there is no such thing. If we look at the waste, brutality, and catastrophes of the natural world, as well as the ignorance, cruelty, violence, torment, murder, and horror that wrack so much of human history, we may indeed be overwhelmed by the misery and apparent absurdity of existence. Hence we may be inclined to think that whatever harm people do, it is not their fault; they are just the victims of this whole process.

However, if a person is nothing more than a puppet dangling helplessly and hopelessly from the strings of physical, psychic, and historical forces, then the very person and all his or her dignity is gone. In such a view, human tragedy is only dust in the wind. There is a person only if there is a "someone" to whom these influences or events happen, a unique center of awareness and freedom who undergoes and responds to them. If we are to talk of a person at all, and not just an impersonal sea of conflicting forces, there must be such a unique center. It is distinct from all these forces, and they do not have access to it. In the obscurity of this inner sanctuary a person freely decides about himself or herself and about life. The presence before whom he decides is what is meant by "God."

The inner sanctuary or core of the person is surrounded by many layers, however; and influences from outside do have access to these layers. Our fundamental decision at the core will seek to express itself in the rest of our makeup and in our outward actions. But it can meet resistance, and then the more outward attitudes and actions refract and distort rather than reflect the decision of the heart. In other words, inner disposition and outer appearance are often not in harmony. For example, we commonly express friendship by a handshake, but this sign is obviously impossible for a person who has lost both arms. Similarly, if a person has suffered injury to his or her emotional life, a sincere desire for friendship may be thwarted by an unfree fear of being hurt, so the fear comes out as aloofness or sarcasm.

The same psychic state or conduct can thus spring from a free act or from unfree conditioning. The layers of our being are the meeting ground, and even the arena, of struggle: between freedom from within and compulsion from without. Certain states of mind may be produced, for example, either by inner discipline or by drugs. It may be difficult to tell whether something negative is our own doing or a burden imposed upon us, whether we are more in need of forgiveness or of healing. Do we truly seek friendship but feel compelled by the fear of hurt to build defensive walls? Or do we freely reject others and use that fear as a pretext for the walls we really wish to build?

We move, then, to a notion of sin as a free negative act at the core of our being, which reaches out to put its stamp upon our whole self and our environment in attitudes and actions which are destructive to self and others. We might at first suppose that no one would freely act in this way. However, if there are conscious and free centers and if there is destructive behavior, we can, in theory, imagine the two as being deliberately linked. More practically speaking, we are aware of our own destructive tendencies and of our own responsibility, and we sense uneasily that these too may be somewhat linked. We may even sense with a shudder that there is also something in us that is strangely attracted to the atrocities of history.

How can we further understand the sinful deed and the God it betrays? From what has been said we might suspect that sin will be a fundamental option which decides on meaninglessness, flows into hatred, and ends in despair.

As we have pointed out earlier, we are given into our own hands and called to fashion and bestow ourselves. That from which we flow as precious gift, before which we are accountable, and by which we are called, is what is meant by "God." A negative act of freedom would be one of refusal, a rejection of the gift and call, and so of their ultimate ground. Sin is an act at the core of our being which denies who we really are.

Insofar as we are gift, sin is a spurning of the gift and its source. We can spurn both gift and source in three inter-related ways. We can refuse to acknowledge our finiteness and contingency. Or we can do so but regard ourselves as mere fluke. Or we can recognize the gift but resent it and regard it as of little value. In the first way we try to see ourselves as infinite, to make ourselves the center of everyone and everything, and so perhaps seek to dominate all within our reach. In the second instance a sense of utter pointlessness pervades our existence. In the third case we live a life filled with resentment, self-hatred, and anger.

All three flow together. We cannot long maintain our pretense to infinity; this pretense readily gives way to a sense of futility or resentment at our own finiteness. In the end, if we are finite, we are either of no meaning and worth or we have these as gift. We cannot be our own gods, and we tend to resist and dislike this fact. Sin is a saying no to this truth from our inmost core. It is a saying no that is free, in the face of a truth we at least dimly and implicitly grasp. To choose the path of sin is to live a lie and deny our true self. In the light of the perspective developed throughout this book, the presence to whom we utter this no is what is meant by "God."

If we reflect, we are aware that we are drawn in this negative direction. The dark side of our longing for the infinite is our dissatisfaction with our own finiteness. This dissatisfaction pushes us toward hostility to the gift and its source. Note, for example, how difficult it is to accept a gift graciously.

Insofar as we are also called to fashion and bestow our gift, sin is a refusal of that call and goal. If the call resides in our longing for "something more," the refusal dwells in our stopping short at something less. It means we have taken the core option of making something finite into an infinite. Whereas the other pole is a refusal to accept our own finiteness, this pole is a refusal to accept the finiteness of something else. We try to find the total fulfillment of our longing in a thing, person, or institution, whether money or pleasure, marriage or family, nation or economic system. We demand that this be our God. In this case, too, we demand of someone or something more than it can give. Our gods fail, and they leave a trail of futility and hostility in their wake.

Nothing that is finite can be our God. Sin is a rejection of this truth from the core of our being. It is a saying no against our conscience, against the best that we know or dimly glimpse. It means that we choose to live a lie and deny the truth of the other. That to whom we utter this no is what is meant by "God."

We are likewise aware that we are drawn in this negative direction. One aspect of our longing for the infinite is that it always lies beyond our grasp. Its elusiveness thrusts us toward resenting the call and its source and then seizing upon and settling for something within our grasp. Note, for instance, how frequently we are disappointed after we have finally acquired some longed-for object or entered into a relationship with some person.

Moreover, the gift and call come to us as to unique persons. Hence we say no in the face of an utterly personal gift and call. We deny what we sense to be our truest identity and our uniquely personal vocation. The experience of sin is much more than merely breaking a law or even performing a morally wrong action in isolation. It is the sense that we have somehow been untrue to our own inmost truth, that we have betrayed the best that is in us, that we have missed our real vocation. We are aware that we have done so and are accountable.

Sin is here seen much more clearly as the betrayal of a unique gift and calling conferred upon us and dependent upon us alone. It is a betrayal of a sacred trust. That which we touch upon as ultimately betrayed is what is meant by "God." Sin is better understood as personal betrayal and rejection than as law-breaking. God is that ultimate trust-worthiness which we thereby violate.

Along these lines, for example, we may be caught up short and see how our lives are following a path of petti-ness, illusion, compromise, and falsehood. We may sud-denly see more deeply into another person and recognize how our own indifference, unconcern, self-preoccupation, and anger have shackled our caring and inflicted pain. In such cases the falling short is painfully real, although the degree of freedom is hard to ascertain.

Sin is thus a core act which concerns the shape of our self and of our life as a whole. We decide who we are, however, in the face of the things, persons, communities, and insti-tutions which make up our environment. We seek to impress this decision upon the rest of our makeup and our environment. Sin will, therefore, express itself in the violation of the gifted sacredness of others. In terms of the above discussion we might say that sin will flow into the treatment of others as idols, as meaningless, or as value-less. In so doing, sin will drain their life, throw it away, or trample it. It will try to kill something in the other in a variety of ways, whether individually or institutionally.

An inevitable effect of sin is suffering. Sin is a clash

between who we really are and who we choose to be. It vents itself in attitudes and actions destructive to self and others. Still, it is not easy to tell the difference between what we freely do and what we are afflicted by and driven to do. Beneath the debris of wrong and hurt and tragedy we find the person who has been wounded by them. But we also find the person who has helped to inflict them. To some degree we find in ourselves and others both the wounded person who needs healing and the violating person who needs forgiveness. In either case there is a putting to death in some form.

Where do we find life out of this death? We find it in the person or community which forgives and heals. This is what the Church is intended to be. Behind this presence we discern an infinite presence, an ultimate source of and summons to forgiveness and healing. This too is what is meant by "God." Let us first look at forgiveness and then at healing.

To utter a final no to the source and goal of all, to freely betray our true self, to violate another, and to unleash all the distress that follows—this is indeed a terrible and terrifying thing to do. How can we possibly admit that in our inmost sanctuary we may have been false, that a shadow of wrongness darkens our entire life, that we have trampled upon what is precious and beautiful? We cannot do so unless we experience that wrongness and brokenness within a context of forgiveness. Otherwise it is too devastating to contemplate, and it can only hurl us into despair.

We can admit our wrong only if it is forgiven. We can change and grow beyond our wrong only if we admit the wrong. In the experience of being enabled to admit our betrayal without despair and of being challenged to grow beyond it we touch upon God as ground of forgiveness. That which ultimately forgives us, reveals our sin, and calls us to new life beyond this death is what is meant by "God."

How can we understand forgiveness? Usually we admit something negative to another only if we trust that he or she will not reject us for it. We hope the other will value and perhaps reassure us despite the blemish. In fact, we can admit something to ourselves only if it does not tear away our last shred of self-esteem. The only escape from illusion or deceit is the hope that our whole identity is not bound up with this wrong, in our own or another's eyes. Otherwise we hide behind denial, excuses, and shifting the blame to others.

A reverse illustration shows the matter clearly. In a heated argument people sometimes try to score points by dragging in a negative incident from the past. There is more to this than raising an item which cannot be disputed. One individual is saying that he or she still holds this past action against the other. Even more, one is implying that the other can never escape this deed, is forever tied to it, identified with it.

To refuse to forgive is to say that a person is trapped in his or her past action and is helpless to escape. This attitude is also found in the wider social sphere. We trot out the alleged misdeeds of another nation as a basis of condemnation now and forever into the future. We envisage no possibility of going beyond the present stalemate. At the same time, we loudly proclaim our own innocence, and the cycle of illusion, deceit, denial, excuses, and shifting of blame is initiated.

To forgive another is to proclaim a worth in that person

which goes deeper than any guilt. It is to invite a person to grow beyond that wrong. In forgiving we call a person to a new life which is in harmony with his or her true worth and that of others.

In our deepest experience of wrongness within ourselves we may find it possible to hope. If so, we are hoping that our worth is not destroyed by this wrong but that we may be forgiven and find a renewed and healed life. That which enables and summons us to this hope is what is meant by "God." In the experience of human worth we touch upon the ultimate source of that worth. To experience that this worth is deeper than sin and not destroyed by it is to experience its ultimate source as forgiving. In this vein, to repent is not to proclaim that we are no good; rather, it is to promise gratefully to live according to a worth which remains despite our betrayal.

It is sometimes said that we live in an age which no longer believes in sin, an age which claims that God is dead. Perhaps we might more accurately say that we live in an age which finds it difficult to believe in forgiveness. Horrible things have happened in our century. Wars between nations and upheavals within them have brutalized, maimed, and destroyed countless numbers of persons in mind and body. Such events create anxiety and erode our ideas of innocence and inevitable progress. It is difficult, on the one hand, to accept a shared responsibility for any of these evils and, on the other hand, to avoid seeing in them the essence of life. To believe that we cannot be forgiven and to believe that the final truth about life is its harsh and unforgiving character are of a piece. Such beliefs show up in defensiveness, mistrust, and harshness on intimate personal and larger social levels. Perhaps one of the most crucial and

practical needs of our time is to believe in the possibility of
forgiveness as ultimate, and consequently to believe in a
human worth which remains despite scars on our individual lives and on our history.

Sin, in its deepest sense, is a commitment and way of life
which denies our true self, violates the worth of others, and
betrays their ultimate source. Forgiveness recognizes a
worth which persists despite the sin, and it summons us to
new life out of this death. Out of sin comes suffering. Out
of forgiveness comes healing. Let us now consider both
suffering and healing a little more closely.

Sin sets up a contradiction between who we really are
and who we choose to be. The decision of our heart
contradicts our heart's deepest orientation. Our refusal of
"something more" contradicts our longing for that "something more," for the infinite. This collision is painful. It is
as if we should refuse to recognize our need for food. The
engulfing pain of hunger will express the contradiction
between choice and reality. Insofar as sin is a free act of our
core it entails suffering as an intrinsic consequence. It
denies a gift and call, a worth and longing, which do not go
away but instead make their presence painfully felt.

This inner decision tries to impress itself upon the rest of
our self and our environment. This expression again involves actions which deny our own and others' worth as
unique persons and the dimensions of our human makeup.
This violation causes suffering. Physical pain, the most
obvious instance, conveys the body's resistance to mistreat-
ment. It is a sign that something is amiss. The same is true
of the pain of emotional abuse and, in general, of the
suffering that arises from being treated as of little or no
value. When damage is inflicted upon any part or dimen-

sion of our person, we protest and resist. Whether the damage is done by or to ourselves, the conflict between how we act or are treated and who we are is painful. Here, too, there is a clash between action and reality.

The harmful effects may continue long after the original intention is withdrawn or changed. The physical pain continues in another even if we regret striking him or her. Most people who batter their children received the same treatment themselves as children. Even if the original damaging act was not free, but accidental or compulsive, its effects are obviously felt.

Suffering is an intrinsic consequence of sin because sin is a decision and action that contradicts one's own and others' true reality. Sin radiates a circle of suffering from the core of the sinner into his or her makeup and environment and even into the future.

We can picture such circles extending over space and time, across our world and throughout human history. Without our choice, we are born into a situation which reflects the harmful deeds of ages and places past. We come into an age and society and family which are wounded and which wound us in turn, and we pass these wounds on to others. Our human heritage has, of course, many positive, creative, healing, life-giving elements, as we have already stressed. The issue here is that much of the suffering we and others undergo does not spring from our own decisions or from those of others around us but from the concrete human situation into which we are born. This situation impels us to further harmful attitudes and actions in which our freedom and even to some degree our awareness play little or no part.

As a consequence, we cannot readily identify people's

suffering with their own personal sin. To view suffering as a punishment from God is an arrogance which neither the book of Job nor the cross of Christ nor the events of the twentieth century can countenance. Can we make any connection between sin and punishment if we think only of the basic core option and do not try to determine who might be guilty of a particular free act?

In trying to establish a connection between sin and punishment, we need not think of God as a civil judge passing judgment on an offence and then assigning a penalty. Likewise, we need not picture God as a judge who intervenes from without to punish people who disobey his arbitrary commands. Even aside from the questionableness of the image itself, in such a view what makes an action sinful is simply God's arbitrary decision, and the connection between God, sin, and punishment comes after the fact of sin. But there is a more intrinsic connection between God, sin, and punishment. Actually, the question of what constitutes a sin is bound up with who God is and who we are, and the painful consequences of sin (the punishment, if you will) flow from the sinful act itself rather than being imposed arbitrarily from the outside.

If we remain within the experience of sin itself, we see this core option as self-destructive insofar as it violates our own self as well as others. Hence punishment is something contained within the act itself. When a child places a hand on a hot stove, for example, the pain is not an added punishment; it is implied in the action itself. When we use our freedom to deny our unique worth, our humanity, our orientation to love and community, our outreach to the infinite, this too hurts; we experience the pain of self-betrayal. Physical pain or emotional anxiety is a sign that something needs attending to. Similarly, the inner pain of sin is a sign that something inside us needs attending to. It points to the violation of our precious gift and unique call. But this gift and call remain even though they have been negated. They persist through the pain as a summons to a new core decision, a change of heart or conversion which will correspond to our true identity and vocation.

To experience this painful contradiction and call is also to experience God. We touch upon God here as the ultimate ground of our continuing sacredness despite our sin, and as the summons to begin to live anew according to our worth. In the gift of acknowledging our wrongness and changing our heart's decision so that we may be open to receive forgiveness and the healing of our ravaged nature, we touch upon God.

We find here as well a further dimension of what is called the fidelity or immutability of God, one which the prophet Hosea discovered out of his own life situation. To experience our enduring worth and meaning despite wrongness within us is to encounter an infinite trustworthiness stronger than any betrayal of trust, an infinite source of life deeper than any taking of life. That to which we are enabled and summoned to entrust ourselves, even out of the brokenness within, is what is meant by "God."

If we are able really to grasp the idea that sin is self-destructive, then we may come to see it more as an occasion of compassion than of condemnation. We may see sin as a challenge to bring to life even out of death rather than to put further to death. This is all the more so inasmuch as it is hard to discern what in our pain is choice and what is burden. There are far-reaching social as well as more intimate personal and interpersonal ramifications here. If all wrong, suffered or inflicted, is a denial of human worth, then all reversal of this direction implies an affirmation of worth in self and others, despite the violations. It means, in other words, forgiveness as we have defined it. This does not mean that we should immediately open all prisons and destroy all armaments. It does mean that we should question the effectiveness of approaches and policies geared to demean, humiliate, or injure another person or group. It also suggests that perhaps we should look within to discover whether any degree of self-righteousness and vindictiveness we find there may not mask a self-hatred which does not believe in forgiveness for ourself. It is indeed very difficult to believe in forgiveness for ourself. That which enables and summons us to do so and to reflect that belief in our lives is what is meant by "God."

What can we make of the wider suffering which pervades human history, of which people seem to be the victims more than the agents? We cannot look for some magical answer from outside. Once again, we can simply ask whether or not we are still able and challenged to reach out of despair into hope, and out of cynicism and indifference to caring about the wounds of others. If so, we proclaim our belief in a final source and goal of meaning despite tragedy.

To some degree, we are all wounded inside and live in a broken world. We need not only forgiveness but healing. If the effect of sin is wounding, then the reversal of sin and its consequences is a process of healing.

The first step in this reversal, and a continuing one, has already been mentioned: conversion. In the sense used here, conversion is not a surface emotional experience or even a deeper one. Rather, it is a reversal of the fundamental option at the core of one's being. Such a profound change in a person's free decision as to who he or she is, a change from rejection to response, can be experienced only as gift. It will be a gift contained within the gift of forgiveness, revelation of sin, and summons to new life beyond this death. The experience of God in this context is the experience that, without ceasing to be responsible and accountable, we are somehow accepted, valued, loved, forgiven, healed in the core of our being, and summoned to total trust despite our brokenness and betrayal.

Conversion is a new decision of the heart in response to the infinite mystery experienced as forgiving love. The challenge and task of authentic conversion is to extend progressively that core decision into every layer of our makeup and out into our physical, intimately personal and interpersonal, and wider social environment. This is the ongoing process of healing. It coincides with the process of gathering and giving the self individually and socially, with the hope of enduring meaning. Yet it brings out a new element. This process meets with the resistance of the brokenness and wrongness which remain in ourselves, in others, and in our social contexts.

The gathering of self must struggle against ingrained dispositions, stubborn attitudes, insistent impulses, and deep-seated conflicts. It is in some ways a gathering of broken pieces. The gift of self to another must contend with tensions, divisions, hostility, and the like. It is always in some sense a reconciliation. The building of a new society must ever struggle with the elements in institutions and structures that tend to dehumanize and alienate.

This process of healing and fulfillment is slow, painful, and never complete during one's lifetime. As with the reality of death, it brings home to us in a vivid way the incompleteness of life and our inability to abolish all sorrow. It makes clear our finiteness. This finiteness is nonetheless seen in the light of the infinite toward which we tend. Our outreach from the heart is thus in part a reaching out of wrongness, woundedness, and incompleteness for a forgiveness, wholeness, and fullness of life which can only come as gift. That which sustains this hope and toward which it reaches is what is meant by "God."

We return to the image of the last chapter: that of one human being representing all human beings—one who accepts the gift of all into his hands, transforms it by his vision, love, and hope, and raises it in offering. We picture this one person as Jesus. But it is clear now that the transformation and the offering take place on a cross. And in him is uttered the final word of life: "Father, into your hands I commend my spirit" (Luke 23:46).

# CONCLUSION

# The Gift of Hope

"Where is your God?" This is the question with which we began our inquiry. We have translated it into a number of other questions: What is my worth? What is my responsibility? Where do I belong? What is my goal? What do I do with my pain? What do I do with my wrong? These are the questions which lie beneath the surface of our whole lives—beneath all that we think, feel, say, and do.

They also echo a still-deeper question. Is it possible to live with hope? Is it possible to live with hope, in spite of evil? If we may do so, without illusion or pretence, we are indeed grateful. Hope is both gift and challenge. The source and goal of this gift and challenge is what is meant by "God."

Beneath all our questions is a longing from the heart. This longing really defines us as persons. We are outreach from the core. To hope is to experience that our longing is not in vain. We gradually gather up into our hands our whole selves, our lives, and our world, in all their brokenness and beauty. We look for somewhere to entrust them. If there is hope, that from which we receive them and to which we entrust them is God.

The question of God is not an idle curiosity about the existence of one possible being. It is a life-and-death question about the possibility of hope. In pursuing this question we have tried to avoid two extremes: that of divorcing God from human experience, and that of reducing God to human experience. We have said, rather, that God is what we touch upon in our deepest human experience. But what we touch upon is totally other. In Christian terms, this presence within which is totally other is embodied in the man Jesus.

We have also focused upon the two poles of our experience: our inmost core and our furthest outreach. These are our points of contact with God. The more immediately "practical" significance of the question of God should also be clear. A balance of solitude and involvement, a strong sense of worth, and a belief in forgiveness, for example, have immense repercussions on our intimate inner and interpersonal lives as well as on our broader societal lives.

In writing this book, one aim has been to deepen our understanding of God, to relate it more fully to lived experience, and to emphasize its social implications. This is especially necessary for those who remain within religious traditions. For those who do not, our aim has been both to invite them to reflect on their own experience and to offer them a fresh approach to the basic questions about life that religion poses. For those who are not content with either glib answers or ready dismissals, who seek to be true to their deeper experience and insights, we have tried to articulate some alternatives.

Most important, our aim has been to help deepen the sense of hope in all who read this book.

# Bibliography

It seemed best, for the purposes of this book, to arrange the bibliographical items chronologically rather than alphabetically. Within each subdivision the order is: books, periodical articles, encyclopedia articles.

## Works of Karl Rahner

Part One

*Theological Investigations,* Vols. 1-14, 16. London: Darton, Longman & Todd; New York: Seabury Press, 1961-1979.

*Do You Believe in God?* New York: Paulist Press, 1969.

*Christian at the Crossroads.* New York: Seabury Press, 1975.

*Foundations of Christian Faith: An Introduction to the Idea of Christianity.* New York: Seabury Press, 1978.

*Our Christian Faith: Answers for the Future.* New York: Crossroad, 1981.

*Encyclopedia of Theology: The Concise Sacramentum Mundi.* New York: Seabury Press, 1975.

"The Concept of Mystery in Catholic Theology," *Theological Investigations* 4:36-73.

"The Theology of the Symbol," *Theological Investigations* 4:221-252.

"Thoughts on the Possibility of Belief Today," *Theological Investigations* 5:3-22.

"The Man of Today and Religion," *Theological Investigations* 6:3-20.

"Observations on the Doctrine of God in Catholic Dogmatics," *Theological Investigations* 9:127-144.

"Atheism and Implicit Christianity," *Theological Investigations* 9:145-164.

"The Experience of God Today," *Theological Investigations* 11:149-165.

"Experience of Self and Experience of God," *Theological Investigations* 13:122-132.

"Christianity" and "Mystery" in *Encyclopedia of Theology,* pp. 188-202, 1000-1004.

Part Two

Chapter 5

*Encounters With Silence.* New York: Newman Press, 1960.

*On Prayer.* New York: Paulist Press, 1968.

*Christian at the Crossroads.* New York: Seabury Press, pp. 48-74.

"Thoughts on the Theology of Christmas," *Theological Investigations* 3:24-34.

"Christian Living Formerly and Today," *Theological Investigations* 7:3-24.

"Mysticism" and "Prayer" in *Encyclopedia of Theology,* pp. 1004-1011, 1268-1277.

Chapter 6

*Grace in Freedom.* London: Burns & Oates; New York: Herder and Herder, 1969, pp. 203-264.

*Meditations on Freedom and the Spirit.* New York: Seabury Press, 1978, pp. 31-71.

"The Dignity and Freedom of Man," *Theological Investigations* 2:235-263.

"Theology of Freedom," *Theological Investigations* 6:178-196.

"Institution and Freedom," *Theological Investigations* 13:105-121.

Chapter 7

"On the Question of a Formal Existential Ethics," *Theological Investigations* 2:217-234.

"The 'Commandment' of Love in Relation to the Other Commandments," *Theological Investigations* 5:439-459.

"Reflections on the Unity of the Love of Neighbor and the Love of God," *Theological Investigations* 6:231-249.

"Christian Humanism," *Theological Investigations* 9:187-204.

"Marriage as a Sacrament," *Theological Investigations* 10:199-221.

Chapter 8

*On the Theology of Death.* Freiburg: Herder; Montreal: Palm, 1961.

*Foundations of Christian Faith.* New York: Seabury Press, 1978, pp. 431-447.

"The Life of the Dead," *Theological Investigations* 4:347-354.

"On Christian Dying," *Theological Investigations* 7:285-293.

"On the Theology of Hope," *Theological Investigations* 10:242-259.

"Ideas for a Theology of Death," *Theological Investigations* 13:169-186.

## Chapter 9

"Christianity and the 'New Man,'" *Theological Investigations* 5:135-153.

"The Experiment with Man," *Theological Investigations* 9:205-224.

"Immanent and Transcendent Consummation of the World," *Theological Investigations* 10:273-289.

"The Peace of God and the Peace of the World," *Theological Investigations* 10:371-388.

"The Church's Commission to Bring Salvation and the Humanization of the World," *Theological Investigations* 14:295-313.

"On the Theology of Revolution," *Theological Investigations* 14:314-330.

## Chapter 10

*Foundations of Christian Faith.* New York: Seabury Press, 1978, pp. 90-115.

"Guilt and Its Remission: The Borderland Between Theology and Psychology," *Theological Investigations* 2:265-281.

"The Comfort of Time," *Theological Investigations* 3:141-157.

"Guilt—Responsibility—Punishment within the View of Catholic Theology," *Theological Investigations* 6:197-217.

"Does Traditional Theology Represent Guilt as Innocuous as a Factor in Human Life?" *Theological Investigations* 13:133-151.

"Contrition," "Conversion," and "Sin" in *Encyclopedia of Theology,* pp. 288-291, 291-295, 1586-1590.

See also J. Norman King, *The God of Forgiveness and Healing in the Theology of Karl Rahner.* Washington: University Press of America, 1982.

For a basic collection of Rahner's writing, see *A Rahner Reader,* ed. Gerald McCool. New York: Seabury Press, 1975.

For an introduction to Rahner's theology as a whole, see *A World of Grace: An Introduction to the Themes and Foundations of Karl Rahner's Theology,* ed. Leo O'Donovan. New York: Seabury Press, 1980.

# Works by Other Authors

Baum, Gregory. *Man Becoming: God in Secular Experience.* New York: Herder and Herder, 1970.

Berger, Peter. *A Rumor of Angels.* Garden City, N.Y.: Doubleday, 1969.

Boros, Ladislaus. *Meeting God in Man.* Garden City, N.Y.: Doubleday, 1971.

_____. *Hidden God.* New York: Seabury Press, 1973.

Evans, Donald. *Faith, Authenticity, and Morality.* Toronto: University of Toronto Press, 1980.

Gilkey, Langdon. *Naming the Whirlwind: The Renewal of God-Language.* Indianapolis: Bobbs-Merrill, 1969.

Kaufmann, Gordon. *God the Problem.* Cambridge: Harvard University Press, 1972.

Küng, Hans. *Does God Exist? An Answer for Today.* Garden City, N.Y.: Doubleday, 1980.

McBrien, Richard P. *Catholicism,* Vol. 1. Minneapolis: Winston Press, 1980.

Murray, John Courtney. *The Problem of God: Yesterday and Today.* New Haven: Yale University Press, 1964.

Ogden, Schubert. *The Reality of God and Other Essays.* New York: Harper and Row, 1964.

Robinson, John A. T. *Honest to God.* London: SCM Press, 1963.

_____. *Exploration into God.* London: SCM Press, 1967.

Schilling, S. Paul. *God Incognito.* Nashville: Abingdon Press, 1974.

Shea, John. *Stories of God: An Unauthorized Biography.* Chicago: Thomas More, 1978.

Smith, John E. *Experience and God.* New York: Oxford University Press, 1968.